WHAT THE CRITICS SAY:

A very worthwhile addition to any travel library. —WCBS Newsradio

Armed with these guides, you may never again stay in a conventional hotel.
—Travelore Report

Easily carried ... neatly organized ... wonderful. A helpful addition to my travel library. The authors wax as enthusiastically as I do about the almost too-quaint-to-believe Country Inns. —San Francisco Chronicle

One can only welcome such guide books and wish them long, happy, and healthy lives in print. —Wichita Kansas Eagle

This series of pocket-sized paperbacks will guide travelers to hundreds of little known and out of the way inns, lodges, and historic hotels.... a thorough menu.
—(House Beautiful's) Colonial Homes

Charming, extremely informative, clear and easy to read; excellent travelling companions. —Books-Across-The-Sea *(The English Speaking Union)*

...a fine selection of inviting places to stay... provide excellent guidance....
—Blair & Ketchum's Country Journal

Obviously designed for our kind of travel.... [the authors] have our kind of taste.
—Daily Oklahoman

The first guidebook was so successful that they have now taken on the whole nation.... Inns are chosen for charm, architectural style, location, furnishings and history. —Portland Oregonian

Many quaint and comfy country inns throughout the United States... The authors have a grasp of history and legend. —Dallas (Tx.) News

Very fine travel guides. —Santa Ana (Calif.) Register

A wonderful source for planning trips. —Northampton (Mass.) Gazette

...pocketsize books full of facts.... attractively made and illustrated.
—New York Times Book Review

Hundreds of lovely country inns reflecting the charm and hospitality of various areas throughout the U.S. —Youngstown (Ohio) Vindicator

Some genius must have measured the average American dashboard, because the ~~Complete Traveler's Companion~~ it right between the tissues and bananas on our ~~...~~ books with good-looking photographs.... very

—East Hampton (N.Y.) Star

ALSO AVAILABLE IN THE COMPLEAT TRAVELER SERIES

- ☐ Europe by Eurail: *How to Tour Europe by Train*

- ☐ Britain by Britrail: *How to Tour Britain by Train*

- ☐ America by Train: *How to Tour America by Rail*

- ☐ Bed & Breakfast America: *Great American Guest House Book*

- ☐ National & State Parks: *Lodges, Cabins, & Resorts*

- ☐ **Country Inns** & Historic Hotels of Great Britain

- ☐ **Country Inns** & Historic Hotels of Canada

- ☐ **Country Inns** & Historic Hotels of Ireland

- ☐ **Country** New England **Inns**

- ☐ **Country Inns** & Historic Hotels of the Middle Atlantic States

- ☐ **Country Inns** & Historic Hotels of the South

- ☐ **Country Inns** & Historic Hotels of the Midwest & Rocky Mts.

- ☐ **Country Inns** & Historic Hotels of California & the Northwest

- ☐ Guide to Country New England

- ☐ Guide to California & Pacific N.W.

- ☐ Guide to Texas and the Southwest

- ☐ *Scheer's* Guide to Virginia

- ☐ *Scheer's* Guide to North Carolina

- ☐ *Scheer's* Guide to Tennessee

- ☐ *Scheer's* Guide to Florida

If your local bookseller, gift shop, or country inn does not stock a particular title, ask them to order directly from Burt Franklin & Co., Inc., P.O. Box 856, New York 10014, U.S.A. Telephone orders are accepted from recognized retailers and credit-card holders. In the U.S.A., call, toll-free, 1-800-223-0766 during regular business hours. (In New York State, call 212-627-0027.)

Ireland

COUNTRY INNS
Castles & Historic Hotels

Eileen O'Reilly & Eugene O'Reilly

BURT FRANKLIN & COMPANY, INC.

Published by
BURT FRANKLIN & COMPANY
P.O. Box 856
New York, New York 10014

NINTH EDITION

Copyright © 1980, 1983, 1984, 1985, 1986, 1987, 1988,
1989, and 1990 by Burt Franklin [Co., Inc.

Library of Congress Cataloging in Publication Data

O'Reilly, Eileen.
Country inns and historic hotels of Ireland.
(The Compleat traveler's companion)
Includes index.
1. Hotels, taverns, etc. — Ireland — Directories.
I. O'Reilly, Eugene, joint author.   II. Title.
III. Series: Compleat traveler's companion.
TX910.17073   647'.94417
ISBN 0-89102-422-0 (pbk.) 1990

Manufactured in the United States of America

1 3 4 2

Acknowledgments

We want to thank the following: the Irish Tourist Board for help we
received in New York, Dublin, and its regional offices throughout
the Irish countryside, and for pictures borrowed; Dodd, Mead and
Company for permission to use quotations from *In Search of Ireland*
by H. V. Morton; E. P. Dutton and Company, Inc., for permission
to use quotations from "Lovely Is the Lee" and "Sweet Cork of Thee"
by Robert Gibbings; our niece Maureen Rooney for researching the
dates of some quotations.

CONTENTS

Adare • Arklow • Aran Islands • Ballina • Ballinadee • Ballinamore • Ballinascarty • Balllickey • Ballynahinch • Ballyshannon • Ballyvaughan • Bansha • Banteer • Bantry • Blarney • Blessington • Borriskane • Bruckless • Bruree • Cahir • Cappoquin • Carlingford • Carrick-on-Shannon • Carrick-on-Suir • Cashel • Cashel Bay • Castledermot • Ccastlegregory • Castlelyons • Castlerea • Castletownsend • Clifden • Clones • Clonmel • Cloughjordan • Collooney • Cong • Cork • Courtmacsherry • Crossmolina • Crusheen • Dingle • Donegal • Drinagh • Drogheda • Dublin • Dundalk • Dunlavin • Ennis • Feakle • Ferns • Foulksmills • Galway • Glandore • Glen of Aherlow • Glencar • Glin • Gorey • Horse & Jockey • Inistioge • Kanturk • Kenmare • Killarney • Killiney • Killucan • Killybegs • Knocknarea • Knockraha • Lahinch • Letterfrack • Limerick • Lismore • Mallow • Maynooth • Monard • Mountrath • Moville • Muine Bheag • Mullinahone • Navan • Newmarket-on-Fergus • Newcastlewest • Newport • Oughterard • Parknasilla • Prosperous • Ramelton • Rathmullan • Rathnew • Riverstown • Roscommon • Rosslare • Rossnowlagh • Schull • Shanagarry • Sligo • Spiddal • Stokestown • Tahilla • Termonfechin • Thurles • Tralee • Tyrellspass • Waterford • Waterville • Wexford • Wicklow •

LIST OF TOWNS BY COUNTY

Readers interested in visiting a particular county will find it listed below with the names of its towns in alphabetical order as they appear in the text.

Carlow Muine, Bheag.

Clare Ballyvaughan, Crusheen, Ennis, Feakle, Lahinch, Newmarket-on-Fergus.

Cork Ballinadee, Ballinascarty, Ballylickey, Banteer, Bantry, Blarney, Castlelyons, Castletownsend, Cork, Courtmacsherry, Glandore, Goleen, Kanturk, Knockraha, Mallow, Schull, Shanagarry.

Donegal Ballyshannon, Bruckless, Donegal, Killybegs, Moville, Ramelton, Rathmullan, Rossnowlagh.

Dublin Dublin, Killiney.

Galway Aran Islands, Ballynahinch, Cashel Bay, Clifden, Galway, Letterfrack, Oughterard, Spiddal.

Kerry Castlegregory, Dingle, Glencar, Kenmare, Killarney, Parknasilla, Tahilla, Tralee, Waterville.

Kildare Castledermot, Maynooth, Prosperous.

Kilkenny Inistioge.

Laois Mountrath.

Leitrim Ballinamore.

Limerick Adare, Bruree, Glin, Limerick, Newcastle West.

Louth Carlingford, Drogheda, Dundalk, Termonfechin.

Mayo Ballina, Cong, Crossmolina, Newport.

Meath Kilmessan, Navan.

Monaghan Clones.

Roscommon Carrick-on-Shannon, Castlerea.

Sligo Ballymote, Collooney, Knocknarea, Riverstown, Sligo.

Tipperary Ballinderry, Bansha, Borrisokane, Cahir, Carrick-on-Suir, Cashel, Clonmel, Glen of Aherlow, Horse and Jockey, Monard, Mullinahone, Thurles.

Waterford Cappoquin, Lismore, Waterford.

Westmeath Tyrellspass.

Wexford Drinagh, Ferns, Foulksmills, Gorey, Rosslare, Wexford.

Wicklow Arklow, Blessington, Dunlavin, Rathnew, Wicklow.

Ireland

INTRODUCTION

TO THOSE WHO DELIGHT in independent travel we offer this book and wish them happy journeys, sunny adventures, meetings with interesting strangers, and a warm welcome at the end of the day.

Enjoying a lodging is a highly subjective pleasure. We cannot tell you where to go; we can only tell you where we have been and why we have liked it, hoping that you can choose from our descriptions those places that are right for you. Accommodations range from some of the most luxurious hotels in Ireland to modest, relatively inexpensive bed-and-breakfast lodgings, each with its own kind of appeal.

The Irish have been noted throughout the ages for their hospitality. *Céad mile fáilte*, a hundred thousand welcomes, is the traditional greeting when a guest enters a dwelling. Legends from pre-Christian times tell that chieftains of old were expected to entertain every stranger—no questions asked. This spirit of hospitality became a Christian virtue, as it was felt that Christ was in the person of every guest. The sentiment is best expressed in an old poem, translated from the Gaelic:

> Oh King of stars!
> Whether my house be dark or bright,
> Never shall it be closed against any one,
> Lest Christ close his house against me.

The Irishman who discovered he had no food and drink to offer travelers suffered disgrace. If the disgrace was incurred not through the host's negligence but by the fault of one who had agreed to supply him with provisions, the latter was liable, by law, to pay to the one disgraced a "blush" fine *(enech-ruice)* for the mortification suffered.

Although her hospitality is renowned, Ireland has no long tradition of innkeeping. An Irishman who visited England about four hundred years ago told many wonderful tales of his journey. None was more astounding and unbelievable than that in England there were places where the stranger was charged for bed, food, and drink!

For eight centuries Ireland was an occupied and oppressed country. For the first four of those centuries, the English attempted to control all of Ireland, without complete success. Although there were severe laws against their doing so, many of those England sent to settle and rule intermarried with the Irish and adopted local laws, habits, and dress. It has been said they became "more Irish than the Irish." Many names that are thought of today as typically Irish came over to Ireland with the Anglo-Norman invasion, among them Fitzgerald, Fitzsimons, Burke, Walsh, and Dillon. Queen Elizabeth I decided that enough of such nonsense had gone on for four hundred years, and that she would finish the job once and for all. The English poet Edmund Spenser, of *Faerie Queene* renown, himself one of the army of occupation, described a bit of what Queen Elizabeth accomplished in his *View of the State of Ireland*:

> Notwithstanding that the same was a most rich and plentiful country full of corne and cattel, yet, ere one yeare and a half, they were brought to such wretchedness as that any stony heart would rue the same . . . in shorte space there was none almost left, and a most populous and plentiful countrey suddainlie left voyde of man and beast.

This severe state continued for almost another four hundred years. The historian William Lecky wrote, "The suppression of the native race was carried on with a ferocity which . . . has seldom been exceeded in the pages of history."

Understandably, travel in such a society was uncommon except among those who were granted the land from which the native Irish had been driven. They built great mansions and stayed in each other's homes when they traveled about the country. A few hotels were established, especially in Dublin, for their occasional use and for travelers from other nations, but very few hotels in Ireland today are a hundred years old. It is only since 1922, when what is now the Republic of Ireland finally won freedom, that this country has been able to strive for prosperity, upon which the success of hotels depends.

Fortunately for those of us who enjoy experiencing another time as well as another place when we travel, ancient castles, hunting lodges where titled lords once entertained nobility, and Georgian manor houses have been converted to delightful hotels and guest houses. Because Ireland is a small country of about 3.2 million people (Great Britain, for comparison, has a population of about 60 million), and because of its lack of hotel development over the centuries, there are fewer lodgings to choose from here than in larger countries. The beauty of her countryside and the friendliness of her people make Ireland one of the most appealing countries for travelers, and the most attractive hotels are in great demand. When you cannot find room in those, you will need alternatives. If a lodging has interesting public rooms we recommend it even though the bedrooms may be less well decorated than we'd like. We use the term "plain" to describe rooms that are clean and comfortable but not necessarily decorated with style or charm. We also recommend some modern hotels that have a distinct Irish flavor and are set in beautiful countryside. None are the standard roadside motels or large chain-type hotels.

Lodgings in private homes seem to be more popular in Ireland than anywhere else. Travelers who can afford the most expensive hotels often enjoy bed-and-breakfast stays, where they meet friendly people and experience a bit of Irish life. These homes in general are quite plainly furnished. We have tried to find some of the most attractive, especially those in old mansions furnished with some antiques. Don't expect them to look like pictures in *House and Garden* magazine. These were once the homes of the wealthy, but their descendants find it impossible to keep them today in the style to which their ancestors were accustomed.

After some hesitation, we finally decided to criticize certain minor drawbacks here and there, although it seemed not quite "nice" to find fault with some aspects of a pleasant place where the innkeeper was working hard to please. We ourselves, along with other members of our family, are owners of an inn, the Inn at Castle Hill in Newport, Rhode Island. We do not manage it—it is leased—but we are well aware of the hard work required to run an inn successfully. We were told by the author of a guide to American inns never to criticize— just recommend or leave out. But very few, if any, hotels are perfect. We have been disappointed with a lodging, glowingly described in some guidebook, that we might have enjoyed had there not been such a discrepancy between expectation and fact. An overrated place is a letdown, whereas the same place can be enjoyed (or avoided) when the drawbacks are anticipated. We have been pleased with every one of these lodgings, slept in some and eaten in others, and discussed them with other travelers recently returned from similar visits.

We do not name the more than two hundred lodgings that we

checked and found wanting. Some were in once lovely old buildings that were badly modernized; others, though atmospheric, were musty. Even the most dedicated antiquarian finds little romantic about antique smells. Many were adequate but just too "plain."

Although we have taken care to make sure our information is correct, there will inevitably be some changes after this book has gone to press—a hotel closed or sold, opening later or closing earlier in the season, an increase in price. The price category listed should be considered only an indication of the relative cost of the establishment. Rates should always be checked when making reservations.

We look forward to hearing from our readers, who can write to us at P.O. Box 484F, Newport, Rhode Island, 02840—and let us know of their experiences, good or bad, at any of these inns and hotels they may visit. Reader comments are especially helpful to us in keeping track of the performance of each lodging. We would also welcome hearing about our readers' own favorites.

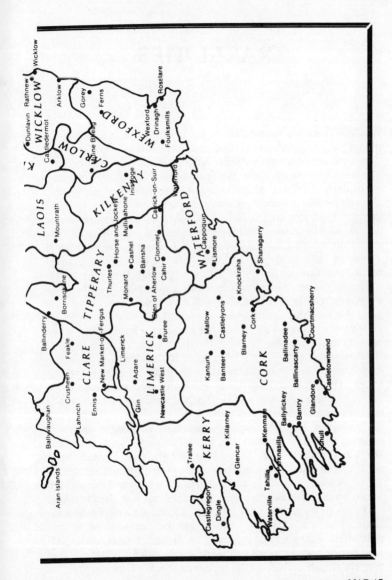

TRAVEL TIPS

IT IS BEST to have a reservation for the first night in any country no matter how much of a vagabond you fancy yourself, and to spend that night no more than 40 miles from the airport, preferably less, if you are hiring a car there. We reserve rooms in advance in a city, particularly in Dublin, which is crowded from May through August. The most attractive places are almost always booked well ahead, and driving and parking are too difficult to allow a search. The night before arrival, we like to stay at a lodging not far away and drive into the city in the morning instead of coping with late-afternoon traffic. If you arrive early in the day and don't like the lodging you have reserved, you can search further before registering. It may be worthwhile for you to change lodgings and lose a deposit. On the other hand, you may be more satisfied with what you have reserved once you have seen the alternatives.

We like to travel to Ireland on Aer Lingus, the Irish airline. When we hear the lilting Irish voices of the flight attendants, we feel that our Irish experience has already begun. It's a thrill to hear the announcement *Céad mile fáilte* (welcome to Ireland) just as the wheels touch ground at the airport. Aer Lingus is the only transatlantic airline that serves both Shannon and Dublin. We sometimes like to land at one airport and depart from the other.

The idea of driving through the countryside, stopping at some cozy little inn when the mood strikes, has a fine romantic lilt to it, and that was the way we wanted to travel. We gradually learned that it is far more romantic to sleep in a four-poster in an ancient castle, where we have reserved in advance, than it is to spend the night in a commercial hotel because everything romantic was already taken.

To ensure an answer when you write abroad for a reservation, include an international reply coupon that you can purchase at your post office. Many hotels, especially small guest houses, cannot afford to pay postage to tell you, and perhaps dozens of others, that they are already full on the dates you require. We find that if we include a deposit in the form of a personal check, we are more likely to secure a reservation. If the lodging cannot take you, it will return the deposit.

We make a few reservations ahead before we leave home if we especially want to stay in some hotels we know to be so highly recommended that they are always booked. We leave nights open between reservations for flexibility and for the unexpected find that might be marvelous. We have learned to start looking for lodging by 3 P.M. Sometimes we find a room in an inn we like on our first try. Sometimes we do not. Then we have time to drive on and seek another. The most unsatisfactory lodgings we have stayed in were the ones we checked into after 5 P.M. By then the charmers are often full. After hearing three or four times that there is no room at the inn, the tendency is to settle for the first clean place that will take you. In season, it is wise to have your hotel telephone ahead for a reservation in some recommended place. A popular hotel is more likely to accept an unsecured reservation from another hotel than from a stranger. Most hotel clerks would be happy to telephone for you, but don't wait until you are checking out to ask, as it can take a while for calls to go through. The local offices of the Irish Tourist Board that are scattered profusely around Ireland (get a list of them from any Tourist Board office) will also telephone to make a reservation. There is a small charge for this service, but you will be given a receipt for a guaranteed reservation. Be sure to telephone and cancel as early as possible if something keeps you from reaching a reserved room, so that it can be rented to someone else. Telephone, also, if you think you will arrive later than expected, so that the room will be held.

One of the easiest ways to save money is to take a room without a private bath. As an innkeeper once said to me, "Most Americans think that taking a room without a private bath is positively *un-American.*" Perhaps they have visions of standing in a hallway dressed in a bathrobe, toothbrush in hand, waiting in line to get into the bathroom. We have never seen, much less experienced, such a scene. There is usually a washbasin in a bedroom without a private bathroom, and there is almost always more than one hall bathroom. In Ireland, unlike some countries in Continental Europe, hall bathrooms are not kept locked, and you do not have to make an appointment or pay to take a bath. Some of the most luxurious hotels in this guide have some rooms without a private bath, and the difference in price can be up to $19 a night.

When asking for a double room, specify whether you will accept a double bed, twin beds, or either. (We have been told, "We have no double room, only one with twin beds.")

Outside of cities, most private homes that take paying guests will serve dinner or a lighter meal called high tea, if they know by about noon that you'll want it. High tea is not afternoon tea, but what Americans would call supper, a substantial three courses; it is always less expensive than dinner.

We suggest you plan to stay about 100 miles from your last lodging. There are no superhighways in Ireland, so you will be on roads that twist and turn. Your actual mileage will be more if you detour to see historic and scenic spots along the way. You may well take time to see a prehistoric ring fort, a folk museum, a stately home, or the ruins of an ancient monastic city or to stop in at a friendly pub or a shop that sells Irish tweed or crystal. If you feel like more driving after you have settled into an inn, there is nothing to prevent you from exploring the surrounding countryside, relaxed in the knowledge that your bags are already unpacked.

We are told, "But I must see as much as possible. I may not get there again." Distances are not important, but quality of experiences is. We find that a stay of about three days in each lodging is ideal. It is delightful to return after a day of sightseeing to join other guests you have already met and to have the staff greet you by name and ask after your day's meandering. Also, many hotels give a reduced rate for a stay of two or more days, usually on the modified American plan (MAP), which includes dinner. Always establish what plan you are taking before registering. If you decide after a day to move on, simply pay the one-day rate and leave. But if after registering for the bed-and-breakfast rate you decide to stay on, you cannot always get the reduced package rate.

The Irish Tourist Board offices in New York and Toronto will send you a list with dates and locations for special events to be held during the year. As well as using such a list to make advance reservations to attend an event, you may also want to use it to avoid being in an area that will be crowded. It would be impossible, for instance, to find attractive last-minute accommodations in Dublin during the annual Dublin International Horse Show in August.

Ireland has become such a popular destination for travelers—a great favorite of those from the Continent—that the most attractive lodgings have far more people wanting to stay in them than can be accommodated. Therefore, we have recommended some places that are suitable for an overnight stay but would not be our first choices for a longer visit. You will need to know of these, both in the most scenic areas—where, because they are crowded in season, it may be difficult to find rooms unless you have booked well ahead—and in sections of the country off the tourist trail through which you may be driving from one destination to another.

Those who would like to read about Ireland and absorb some Irish atmosphere before going might want to subscribe to two publications we enjoy. The first is a magazine, with many photographs in color: *Ireland of the Welcomes* (available in the United States from P.O. Box 2744, Boulder, CO 80322; $12.00 annually for 6 issues). The other is a newsletter and information service—how to buy a house, trace ancestors, find antiques, engage a driver—are answered personally. Subscribers are given vouchers for discounts at many shops and hotels, which will usually more than pay for the subscription: *Inside Ireland* (Rockwood, Ballyboden, Dublin 16, Ireland; $30.00 annually for 4 issues).

SOME THINGS TO
TAKE WITH YOU

Sectional road maps of Ireland. We cannot emphasize too strongly how necessary we feel these to be. Every back road and most small villages are marked. These maps are hard to find in the United States. One source is Book Passage, 51 Tamal Vista Boulevard, Corte Madera, California, 94925, telephone: (800) 321-9785. If you do not bring maps with you, buy them as soon as you arrive. Tourist Board offices, including those at airports, will have them. The Irish Tourist Board office in New York City will send you a free booklet that has a map of all of Ireland, with the most scenic roads outlined.

An electrical converter set, a small, folding high-intensity *lamp,* and an *extension cord.* If you like to read in bed, don't count on a good reading light in every country lodging. Sometimes all you will need is a 75-watt bulb to replace the 25-watt bulb you may find in your bedside lamp. You must buy one when you get to Ireland, as American bulbs do not fit Irish lamp sockets.

Other personal items we have found useful include a *small magnifying glass* to make map reading easier, a *plastic bottle of detergent* (or buy one soon after you arrive), *spot remover,* a *travel clothesline with suction cups, inflatable plastic coat hangers,* a *plastic cleaner's bag* to use under dripping laundry (packed between folds of clothing in your suitcase it helps keep wrinkles away), a roll of *large plastic bags,* a *sewing kit,* a *Buttoneer* for attaching buttons without sewing, a *travel alarm clock,* a *small flashlight,* and *eyeglass and medical prescriptions.*

HOW TO READ
THE LISTINGS

Closed   Unless otherwise noted, lodgings are open all year.

Cocktail bar   The atmosphere of a cocktail bar is more luxurious than that of a public bar. A public bar is heavily patronized by local people.

Credit cards   MasterCard is Accesscard in Ireland.

Dinner   Many hotels serve dinner at noon on Sunday. These usually do not serve snacks or tea on that day.

Easter   Many seasonal hotels reopen for the Easter holidays. Some open the day before Easter Sunday and others a few days earlier.

Fishing   Fishing is listed only for lodgings advising that fishing gear can be rented or borrowed. Many other hotels offer excellent fishing if you bring your own equipment.

Golf   There are a prodigious number of golf courses in Ireland for her size; most of them welcome guests and have golf clubs available, and almost all lodgings are a short drive from a golf course. Therefore, we list golf under recreational facilities only for a hotel that has its own golf course or offers free golf at a nearby course. (We cannot guarantee the quality of the clubs available for use. We have seen some old ones.)

Ground floor rooms   Though not necessarily suitable for guests dependent on wheelchairs, accommodations so labeled are desirable for those who do not want to climb stairs. Never ask for a room on the first floor if you want to be on the ground floor. In Ireland the "first floor" is the floor above the ground floor—what Americans call the second floor.

How to get there	We do not give directions in Dublin or Cork, except to mention if the lodging is near a landmark. Stop and ask directions frequently. When the hotel management will send someone to meet guests at an airport or railway station or will send a taxi to meet them, there will be a charge unless otherwise noted, and arrangements must be made with the hotel when reserving your room.
Hunting	The management will arrange for a guest to join a hunt.
Luncheon	Luncheon is a sit-down meal served in a dining room.
Meals	Every lodging in this guide provide breakfast for house guests.
Price category	Prices can go out of date quickly. We note under the description of each hotel a comparative price rating so the reader can know how it compares in price to the other lodgings in this guide. These prices are for two people in high season and include breakfast (usually a full meal but in a few cases a Continental breakfast), service, and tax. Many lodgings offer lower rates off season. Some lodgings will fall into two categories because some of their rooms are more expensive than others. *Actual rates are listed in the Index,* at the end of this book. Our price categories are in Irish pounds. The approximate exchange rate is: £1 = $1.40.

	Irish Pounds
Very inexpensive	up to £30
Inexpensive	£31–£46
Moderate	£47–£75
Expensive	£76 –£100
Very expensive	over £100

Public bar	See Cocktail bar.
Snacks	A snack is a light meal, usually hot soup and sandwiches, served in a hotel lounge, cocktail lounge, or

sometimes, in good weather, outside. In Ireland, if snacks are served, they are usually served all day and sometimes all evening, though frequently not at all on Sunday.

[T] The lodging will pay a travel agent a commission on rooms. The percentage varies among hotels.

Tea This refers to afternoon tea, including such items as sandwiches, scones, or cake—not just a commercially baked cookie (which is called a biscuit). Frequently tea is not served on Sunday.

Telephone The number in parentheses is the area code. To telephone Ireland from the U.S. or Canada, dial the overseas code, 011, then the code for Ireland, 353, then the Irish telephone number, but eliminate the first 0. For example, to telephone Ariel House, Dublin, (01) 685512, dial 011-353-1-685512.

U.S. Agent Many Irish hotels are represented by the following American agents; you or your travel agent may call these for reservations for the hotels that list an agent in the United States:

Ashford Castle Inc. (800) 346-7007; in New York State and Canada, (212) 957-2700.

Best Western (800) 528-1234; in Phoenix, Arizona, (602) 957-4200.

C.I.E. Tours (800) 243-8687; in New York State, (212) 697-3914.

Quality International (800) 228-5151; in Phoenix, Arizona, (602) 254-9525.

RS (Reservation Systems) (800) 223-1588; in Canada, (800) 531-6767; in New York State, (212) 661-4540.

Robert Reid (800) 223-6510; in Omaha, Nebraska, (402) 498-4307.

Selective Hotels (800) 223-6764; in New York State, (800) 522-5568; in New York City, (212) 714-2323.

THF (Trusthouse Forte) (800) 225-5843.

With bath	Specify if a private bathroom with tub *or* shower is acceptable. (We have been told, "We have no room with a private bath, only one with a shower.") Occasionally a private bathroom must be reached through a public hall. If it is important for you to have a private bath opening directly into your bedroom, specify a bathroom en suite.

ADARE MANOR HOTEL

> Everything about Adare speaks of intelligent interest
> in antique beauty and the desire of preserving it;
> *Stephen Gwynn,* 1927

This antique beauty was for two centuries the home of the Earls of Dunraven. Dating to 1720, the Tudor revival mansion's original interior design includes barrel vaulted ceilings, fifteenth-century Flemish carved doors, ornate marble fireplaces and seventeenth-century choir stalls.

The toweringly high ceilings of this recently opened hotel are adorned with rococo plasterwork. Furnishings are lavish — antique tables, velvet and leather upholstery, Oriental rugs, crystal chandeliers, fine paintings. Some bedrooms are enormous. The atmosphere is friendly, with sometimes asing-song in the Tack Room bar.

The 1000 acre estate contains glorious flower gardens and parkland. Fruits and vegetables served in the hotel are grown organically. Guests can borrow gear to fish for salmon and trout in the River Maigue, which flows through the grounds.

The small town of Adare is considered by many to be the most attractive town in Ireland. As it is only 25 miles from Shannon airport, Adare Manor is the recommended first stop for those headed south who want luxurious lodging.

Price category: Very expensive. *Manager:* Christopher Oakes. *Telephone:* (061) 86566; from the U.S.: (800) 462 3273. *Rooms:* 64 with bath, telephone, and TV; suitable for wheelchair guests. *Meals:* Luncheon, snacks, tea, dinner for public; full license. *Children:* Baby-sitting. *Facilities:* Drawing room, cocktail lounge, garden, laundry service. *Activities:* Golf, indoor pool, trout and salmon fishing, sauna, gym, and bicycles at hotel; riding and hunting nearby. *Credit cards:* Amex, Diners, Master, Visa. *How to get there:* The entrance is on main road as you enter Adare from the north. [T]

WOODLANDS HOUSE HOTEL

> Oh, the vales of old Ireland are pleasant to see
> With their streams and their Woodlands so rare,
> If there's one hallowed spot that is dearest to me
> 'tis the lovely green vale of Adare.
>
> *Joseph M. Crofts*

Here is an inexpensive place for those who prefer a hotel to a private-home lodging. Although it was originally the family farm — the Fitzgeralds still raise beef cattle on 65 acres — a wing of modern bedrooms has been added, along with a cocktail bar and a restaurant with an à la carte menu, where home-cooking and baking are a specialty.

There are some antiques in the entrance hall, but other furniture is modern. It's an informal, friendly place where guests can have tea at any time at no charge. The cocktail lounge has a piano, where a talented guest will play occasionally for a spontaneous singalong.

Adare is one of the prettiest towns in Ireland. As it is close to Shannon airport, Woodlands House is a good first or last stop for the budget traveler.

Price category: Inexpensive. *Proprietor:* Mary Fitzgerald. *Telephone:* (061) 86118. *Rooms:* 12 with bath, TV, and telephone; some suitable for wheel-chair guests. *Meals:* Snacks and tea for guests; dinner for the public; full license. *Children:* Baby-sitting. *Facilities:* TV lounge, cocktail bar, garden. *Activities:* Riding and trout and salmon fishing nearby. *Credit cards:* Amex, Master, Visa. *How to get there:* Driving into Adare from Limerick on Route N20, Woodlands will be signposted. Turn left and find it about a mile along on the right.[T]

ARD EINNE

> Don't read about Aran: go to it! . . . the wide
> unobstructed skies, the Atlantic foaming round the
> rocks, the soft air, the lovely prospect of the Connemara
> hills to the northward, the indefinable charm . . . make
> it a place that, once visited, one never forgets.
>
> *Robert Praeger,* 1937

No, you will not forget the Aran Islands. We stayed on Inishmore, the largest of the three, at Ard Einne, a modern purposely-built guest house run by gracious the Enda Gill. Her husband is principal of the high school, and the family has separate quarters in the house. He is an island native, but Enda is from the east coast of Ireland. They have traveled widely in Europe and worked in Kenya.

As at most so-called bed-and-breakfast lodgings in Ireland, Enda serves dinner too. Her cooking has a reputation for being the best on the island, and we found it very good indeed. Guests sit at separate tables in the dining room. Bedrooms are smallish and neat, with picture windows that look out across stone walls to the sea.

In the living room, with a coal fire in a stone fireplace for chilly evenings, we had a choice of video movies. The one to see is "Man of Aran," a classic made in 1934, a powerful film portraying life on the islands in former times — the dangerous fishing from curraghs during storms, the breaking of rocks to make stone walls, and the hauling of sand and seaweed to make gardens.

When you make your reservation, ask Enda to arrange for a van to meet the boat and bring you to the house, then to return to give you a tour of the island, which has 800 residents, 12 miles of roads, and 7,000 miles of lacy stone walls.

The boat from Rossaveal takes less than an hour, with a free bus from Galway and points in between. Since the trip can be a rough one, one might prefer this trip to the one taking over two hours on the boat from Galway. Or you can fly from Galway. *Price category:* Very inexpensive. *Proprietor:* Mrs Enda Gill. *Telephone:* (099) 61126. *Rooms:* 6 sharing baths. *Meals:* Dinner for guests; wine license. *Facilities:* Living room, garden. *Activities:* Ocean swimming and bicycle rentals nearby. *How to get there:* By boat from Rossaveal or plane from Galway. If you carry just overnight luggage, you can walk to Ard Einne (pronounced Ard Ay nya) from the airport, about a quarter mile away.

WOODMOUNT HOUSE

> I like too, to be in touch with mine host . . . . His local
> interests are of necessity far reaching, and he not only
> knows the country round for many miles, but everybody
> in it.
>
> *Arthur Bradley,* 1903

You'll be in touch with your host here and with his family. The O'Tooles and their four children, most of whom are teen-age or almost so, have a delightful country home.

The house was built about 1790. A marble fireplace and antique accessories enhance the cozy small sitting room, which is comfortable and nicely furnished. Bedrooms are decorated with pretty fabrics and warmed by wall-to-wall carpet. One is very large. The garden is a joy, a fine place to sit and enjoy a cup of tea while admiring the flowers.

Seoirse (Shor' sha, which is Irish for George) raises mushrooms on just one of his eight acres, producing two tons a week. He'll show visitors how its done.

Arklow, a ten-minute walk from the house, was settled by Vikings. When it's time to leave Woodmount, you'll feel you are leaving the home of friends.

Price category: Very inexpensive. *Proprietors:* Maeve and Seoirse O'Toole. *Telephone:* (0402) 32977. *Closed:* Mid September to mid-May. *Rooms:* 4, 1 with bath. *Meals:* Dinner for guests. *Smoking:* Not permitted. *Children:* Not suitable for children under 10. *Facilities:* Sitting room, garden. *Activities:* Grass tennis court at house; ocean swimming nearby. *How to get there:* The house is signposted just north of Arklow on Route N11. Turn onto Beech Road at the large Texaco station. A short way along on the left, find a sign on the gate.

DOWNHILL HOTEL

Price category:
Telephone: (09...
with bath, tel...
fast, lunch...
Children...
ing ro...
gar...
ir...

Oh, the gallant fi...
It is the best of a...
'Tis full of pleas...
And 'tis beloved...

Although the Downhill is renowned for its fishing, it is a...
with many other recreational facilities. It started out as a manor hous...
and has been in the same family for generations. Ann Moylett has preserved the atmosphere of former times in a few of the rooms. When we arrived, guests were lingering over afternoon tea in a drawing room resembling one in a private home. Deep chairs are covered with flowered slipcovers; marble-topped Chinese teak tables hold fresh flowers. Extensive additions have been made to the manor. The spacious window-walled dining room is decidedly purple, a color used much more frequently in Ireland and Britain than in the United States. Standard modern bedrooms are pleasant, decorated with light woods and Irish wool spreads in the natural colors; superior rooms are larger and decorated with floral fabrics. All have good reading lights.

About the fishing — variety is the keynote. The River Moy estuary holds large stocks of sea trout; for example, 103 for one rod for one day's fishing. Princes, lords, and bishops have hauled salmon from the River Moy, which tumbles along over rapids right in front of the hotel. You can join that elite group or take a boat trip out on Lough Conn, one of the best trout and salmon lakes in Ireland. Other lakes and rivers are within easy reach, and all the necessary equipment is available from the hotel. At the Downhill's recreational complex you'll find an attractive oval indoor swimming pool, as well as a squash court, snooker, sauna, Jacuzzi and deck-tennis courts.

We were surprised to find the Downhill such an attractive hotel. We don't know why — perhaps its name did not inspire us. For the traveler who prefers a professional hotel atmosphere with many facilities (there is a gift shop, too), this is certainly one of the most attractive in the northwest. Ireland's President Erskine Childers was a guest twice while in office.

Moderate to expensive. *Proprietor:* Ann Moylett.
21033. *Closed:* Two days at Christmas. *Rooms:* 54
hone, TV, video movies, and tea-making. *Meals:* Break-
n, snacks, tea, supper, dinner for the public; full license.
aby-sitting and -listening; children's meals. *Facilities:* Draw-
, lounge, cocktail bar, public bar, gift shop, beauty salon,
. *Activities:* Indoor pool, deck-tennis, sauna, squash, river fish-
game room, and musical entertainment (except Monday) at the
tel; ocean, lake, and river swimming, riding, hunting, boat trips, and
deep-sea and lake fishing nearby. *Credit cards:* Amex, Diners, Master, Visa. *How to get there:* The hotel is signposted on Route N59 at
the north edge of Ballina (pronounced "Bally na"). Taxis are available
at the Ballina railway station.

MOUNT FALCON

> That man travels to no purpose who sits alone to his
> meals.
>
> *John Davis*, 1802

Constance Aldridge still runs Mount Falcon as if she were having
friends up to the country for a weekend. Neighbors sometimes drop
in and join the group around the fire in the evening, where Con is front
row center, enjoying herself and entertaining her guests. Easy
camaraderie prevails.

All guests sit down to dinner at a long mahogany table, where good
talk is garnished with spontaneous wit. Although you can get a 1959
Chateau Canon-Saint Emilion for £30 a bottle, we found the good wine
that was included with our dinner more than adequate. Just as at a
house party, there was no menu, but everything was excellent, from
smoked salmon appetizer to apricot soufflé followed by a cheese board.
A roast lamb was carved at a sideboard loaded with old silver. An array of Chinese export blue and white platters decorated one wall. From
mid-October on, a fire burns in the dining room at all meals, an especially cheerful sight at breakfast. Butter, vegetables, and honey come
straight from the farm on Mount Falcon's 100 acres. Jam is made in
the kitchen by Con, as is yogurt, with a starter from Yugoslavia and
each succeeding batch started from the one before.

We found the large Victorian entrance hall rather unfriendly look-ing, even forbidding, in early afternoon some years ago, with not a soul around but the maid who let us in. We decided not to stay, and that was our mistake. A year and a half later, having continued to hear good things about Mount Falcon, we came back. Again that enormous hall put us off. But the maid led us into a drawing room with a log fire ab-laze on the hearth and brought afternoon tea on a silver tray; and although neither guests nor hosts had yet appeared, we knew that Mount Falcon was a gracious, friendly place.

Despite such elegant trappings as windows draped with velvet un-der gilt cornices, heavy brass chandeliers hanging from 16-foot ceil-ings, enormous gilt mirrors, and old Oriental rugs, the house is not luxurious. Instead, it is easygoing and comfortable, a bit "reduced coun-try gentleman." No butler appears to take your drink order. The bar is a table in a book-lined alcove where you make your own drinks on the honor system, marking down what you took. Large sofas and chairs are covered with loose cretonne covers. Bedrooms, although spacious and with large old wardrobes, are just a bit austere. Bathrooms have heated towel racks, a nice luxury touch that never seems to have been adopted in the United States. Mount Falcon offers first-class salmon fishing on 7 1/2 miles of the river Moy, with nine ghillies and boats available. Gear can be rented.

We left later than planned next morning. We had lingered over breakfast as the irrepressible Con filled us in on life in Mayo, popping up to toast homemade bread for us on a marble-topped side table. We drove off reluctantly, feeling a bit as if we'd just left an Agatha Christie setting but one without the chills of a murder mystery. Mount Falcon is a place we'd like to stay for some time.

Price category: Moderate to expensive. *Proprietor:* Constance Al-dridge. *Telephone:* (096) 21172. *Closed:* December 22–28 and Febru-ary through March. *Rooms:* 11 doubles with bath; 2 singles sharing a bath. *Meals:* Dinner for public by reservation; full license. *Facilities:* Drawing room, library, garden. *Activities:* Tennis and salmon fishing at the house; indoor pool, sauna, squash, riding, and hunting nearby. *U.S. agent:* Robert Reid Associates. *How to get there:* The inn is sign-posted on N57, four miles south of Ballina (pronounced "Bally na").[T]

Ballinadee, Cork

THE GLEBE HOUSE

> . . . it is yeit a moste beautifull and sweete Country
> as any is under heaven.
>
> *Edmund Spencer,* 1596

This old rectory in the country is owned by Gill Bracken and her husband, Tim, a lawyer in nearby Cork city. A young couple, they both enjoy cooking and share the preparation of the six-course dinner they serve every evening to those who book for it by early afternoon.

Dinner might start with a timbale of tomato and basil, then continue with a fish course of salmon with hollandaise, followed by lemon sorbet. The main course could be lamb with rosemary. Both a cheese tray and dessert end the bountiful meal.

A small but comprehensive wine list is offered. You can take both before- and after-dinner drinks in the sitting room by helping yourself and signing a book.

Bedrooms with antique furniture, mainly Georgian and Regency pieces, have good modern bathrooms. Views are bucolic, looking out on fields where sheep, cattle, and horses graze. Glebe House is near lively Kinsale, one of Ireland's most attractive seaside towns and is a good spot from which to explore the lovely, soft countryside of west Cork's unspoiled coast.

Price category: Very inexpensive. *Proprietors:* Gill and Tim Bracken. *Telephone:* (021) 778294. *Rooms:* 4 with bath. *Meals:* Dinner for guests; wine license. *Facilities:* Living room, library, garden. *Activities:* Riding, ocean swimming, deep-sea and river fishing, sailing, and windsurfing nearby. *How to get there:* From Kinsale take Route R600 west to Ballinspittle, then follow signs for Ballinadee. Guests can be picked up at Cork airport or train station.

GLENVIEW

To me the . . . county of Leitrim conveys a picture
of small mysterious fields, ubiquitous alder bushes and
overgrown little roads. *Bryan MacMahon,* 1971

Guests are made to feel part of the family in Teresa Kennedy's home.
She was a nurse in England before she returned to Ireland to settle down
to life on a farm. When we arrived, she seated us before a fire in a comfortable living room that had a piano and such antique accents as a marble mantle and gleaming brass. Then she brought in tea and delicious
porter cake.

The dining room in the original part of the house, with old china
and brass on white walls and an antique sideboard and chairs, has old-
world charm, but the rest of the house is modern, with showers in the
bathrooms and plain furniture in the bedrooms.

Beside the house there is a picture-book thatched farmhouse you
can rent by the week. Inside are flagstone floors, heavy beams, and an
open fire for turf or logs. Patchwork spreads cover antique beds of brass
and iron in the three bedrooms. An old Irish cupboard holds china in
a kitchen with all modern conveniences. A modern two-bedroom cottage beside it is also available.

Umbrellas shade garden furniture on the lawn, to be used by house
and cottage guests. Both may also have dinner if they let Teresa know
ahead. She'll tell you where traditional Irish music can be heard in local pubs. The Leitrim Heritage Centre in Ballinamore has an index of
all major sources for tracing ancestors in Leitrim.

Price category: Very inexpensive. *Closed:* November through March
except by reservation. *Proprietors:* Brian and Teresa Kennedy. *Telephone:* (078) 44157. *Rooms:* 6, 4 with bath; self-catering cottages by
the week for 6 and for 4. *Meals:* Dinner for guests; wine license. *Children:* Baby-sitting, pony, donkey and cart. *Facilities:* Living room, TV
room, garden. *Activities:* Rowboats at house to take to lake; boat trips
on Shannon River and riding nearby. *How to get there:* From Ballinamore, start south on Route R204, but after you cross the bridge over
the Woodford River, leave R204 and continue straight on. Glenview
House will be on the right. Guests can be met at Dromod train station.

ARDNAVAHA HOUSE HOTEL

He goes not out of his way who goes to a good inn.
Anonymous

Here is a hotel, a favorite of European visitors, that is often overlooked by Americans. "Why this place has everything!" said a young Belgian woman to us. "We came for a night because it is not far from the Cork airport, but we won't leave. We'll do all our touring from here." Indeed, Ardnavaha House is a good center for touring the city of Cork, Killarney, Tipperary, and Waterford and it is near the obligatory Blarney Stone. Golf at a nearby course has a reduction for guests.

The house is set in 40 acres of lawns, woods, and meadows. From the fanlighted doorway, centuries-old trees and rhododendron frame a view that stretches across a wide valley. The original Georgian building, which houses the public rooms, is simply furnished with welcoming red carpet, comfortable upholstered furniture, some antique accessories, and the elaborate silk lampshades that look so fancy to American eyes. All bedrooms are in an attractive modern extension with either a balcony or a terrace. From our terrace we took a moving picture of our daughter cantering across a meadow with heather-covered hills as a backdrop. Even nonriders will enjoy a walk to the clean white stable with its sleek horses and fat, fresh pony.

A swimming pool and terrace in the old courtyard are protected from breezes by the Georgian house and by encircling farm buildings that have been coverted to a sauna and a cocktail lounge. As we sat by the pool one late afternoon, the young chef stopped by to ask the four of us, "Do you like fish? I was just given two pollack, fresh-caught. There is not enough to put on the menu, but I'll cook them for your table if you'd like." Ardnavaha (Irish for a feeling of welcome) is that sort of pleasant, informal place, a hotel of quiet character where people talk to each other.

Price category: Moderate to expensive. *Proprietors:* The Begley Family. *Telephone:* (023) 49135. *Closed:* October to Easter. *Rooms:* 36 with bath and telephone. *Meals:* Luncheon, snacks, tea, dinner for public; full license. *Facilities:* Lounge, TV lounge, card room, garden. *Activities:* Outdoor pool, sauna, riding, tennis, mountain bikes and game room at the hotel; ocean swimming, deep-sea fishing, and sailing nearby. *Credit cards:* Amex, Diners, Master, Visa. *U.S. agent:* Robert Reid Associates. *How to get there:* Ardnavaha is signposted on Route N71 between Clonakilty and Bandon.   [T]

Ballinderry (near Nenagh), Tipperary

GURTHALOUGHA HOUSE

> The inhabitants of this country are very much addict-
> ed to hospitality.
>
> *Tadhg Rody,* 1683

You will find hospitality aplenty at Gurthalougha House, a hotel hidden away on the banks of Lough Derg in a hundred acres of forest

When Bessie and Michael Wilkinson bought this estate, Michael,
a nurseryman, intended to raise trees and shrubs. You'll pass some acres
of nursery stock on the long wooded lane that leads to the house. He
loved to cook, however, and now he is a dedicated chef who turns out
exceptionally good food. Bessie is from a hotel family, her father once
the proprietor of two of Dublin's most renowned hotels, the Royal
Hibernian and the Russell, now gone.

Although the Wilkinsons had to furnish this very large, early nineteenth-century house, they did so by finding appropriate vintage pieces that look as if they've sifted down through generations of good use. Big upholstered couches with loose floral slipcovers and lots of throw pillows are sometimes a bit faded but so comfortable in front of a roaring fire. An interesting mix of antiques — tables, chests, beds, armoires, mirrors, paintings, Oriental rugs — are scattered throughout the large rooms. Guests feel as if they're enjoying a visit to a friend's old family manor. The relaxed attitude here allows breakfast at any time, in bed if you wish.

Some rooms have a view across Lough Derg to the mountains of Clare and Galway. Use the free outboard boat or arrange to have a ghillie take you out on the lake to try for pike, perch, and other coarse fish. The house has a tackle room for visiting anglers. Lough Derg is the largest lake in the Shannon River chain, popular for cruising. See the Shannon boats in nearby Terryglass, where they dock to replenish supplies.

Gurthalougha is a good place for families as there are so many sporting activities to keep everyone busy. We've heard that it's a favorite getaway for dramatist Hugh Leonard.

Price category: Moderate. *Proprietors:* Bessie and Michael Wilkinson. *Telephone:* (067)22080. *Rooms:* 8 with bath; mid-week and weekend breaks. *Meals:* Dinner for the public; wine license. *Children:* Baby-sitting. *Facilities:* Sitting room, library, and garden. *Activities:* Lake swimming, pike, perch, and other coarse fishing and free outboard boat at house; windsurfing, sailing (lessons available), tennis, riding, hunting, and boat trips on the Shannon nearby. *Credit cards:* Amex, Master, Visa. *How to get there:* The house is signposted on Route A493 between Ballinderry and Terryglass. [T]

BALLYLICKEY MANOR

> Were such a bay lying upon English shores it would
> be a world's wonder. If it were in the Mediterranean
> or the Baltic, English travellers would flock to it by
> hundreds.
>
> *William Makepeace Thakeray,* 1842

Overlooking Bantry Bay, whose beauty Thackeray thought neglected, Ballylickey Manor is set amidst ten acres of lawns, flower gardens, and parkland. It was once the hunting lodge of Lord Kenmare, then it became the home of Philip Graves, brother to the writer Robert Graves and at one time foreign editor of *The Times* (London). He had a habit of inviting everyone he knew to come visit, so eventually it seemed natural to turn Ballylickey Manor into a hotel, now owned by George Graves, son of Philip, and his French wife, Christiane.

In the main house are five suites that sleep three each, each with living room, bedroom, and bath. Other bedrooms are in a group of cottages built around a swimming pool, In one cottage are the public rooms — a restaurant and a lounge with a bar at one end — that are decorated with French flair.

The food also has a French accent and is highly lauded by sophisticated guests. This is a particularly nice stop for lunch, whether inside by the fire or, in good weather, beside the pool. Ballylickey Manor is near the borders of Cork and Kerry and is a good center for touring the beauty spots of the west.

Price category: Expensive. *Proprietors:* Christiane and George Graves. *Telephone:* (027) 50071. *Closed:* November to mid-March. *Rooms:* 5 with bath and telephone; 5 suites; ground-floor rooms; 3-day reduction. *Meals:* Luncheon, snacks, tea, dinner for public; full license. *Facilities:* Lounge, garden. *Activities:* Outdoor pool at the hotel; ocean swimming, deep-sea fishing, boat rentals, boat rides, scuba diving, and tennis nearby. *Credit cards:* Amex, Visa. *U.S. Agent:* Robert Reid. *How to get there:* Ballylickey Manor is on the main road in Ballylickey, which is between Bantry and Glengarriff. [T]

SEA VIEW HOUSE

> This northern coast of Bantry Bay is peculiarly magnifi-
> cent. The mountains are . . . very lofty. . . . Their
> outline is most picturesquely broken, their forms
> endlessly diversified. . . .
>
> *J. Belton,* 1834.

Sea View has a really magnificent view—the same enjoyed by Mr Belton more than 150 years ago. The large Victorian House faces Bantry bay, behind a sweep of lawn beautiful with flower beds and garden furniture.

Inside, the rooms are homey rather than stylish, with many antique pieces—here a nice period desk, there a tufted couch. Old pictures enhance the walls, and a wild Victorian overmantel embellishes the cocktail bar. Everything is meticulously cared for, and modern bathrooms are strictly twentieth-century. The three ground-floor bedrooms are in a separate cottage right near the house.

Fresh sea food is a specialty at Sea View, whose dining room is recommended by Michelin. Try the mussels—perhaps in mussel soup—which are "farmed" right in Bantry Bay. Steak was excellent, not always so in Ireland where it is often too well done for American tastes. Later in the evening, tea and cookies were brought round while we were chatting with other guests. From here you can tour Cork City in one direction and Killarney in another.

Price category: Moderate. *Proprietor:* Kathleen O'Sullivan. *Telephone:* (027) 50073. *Closed:* November through March. *Rooms:* 15 with bath; ground floor rooms. *Meals:* Snacks and dinner for public; full license. *Children:* Baby-sitting. *Facilities:* Lounge, TV lounge, cocktail bar, garden. *Activities:* Ocean swimming, deep-sea fishing, boat rental, scuba diving, and tennis nearby. *Credit cards:* Amex, Master, Visa. *U.S. agent:* RS. *How to get there:* Sea View House is on Route N71 between Bantry and Glengariff. [T]

TEMPLE HOUSE

> The first near glance at this delighted us, for it was
> manifest that we had come upon a magnificent . . .
> specimen of architecture of the bygone days when men
> built for themselves grand habitations . . . the lordly
> few of the land, that is.
>
> *James Hissey,* 1889

As we wound up the long driveway, through fields where cattle grazed, the sheer size of Temple House astounded us. We entered another century when we stepped through the front door into its enormous, high-ceilinged entrance hall, decorated with trophies of long-ago hunts and fishing expeditions. A rack on one wall holds rods and waterproof clothes, with waders underneath. On a big center table are guest books signed by visitors who came a century and more ago.

All this might seem very grand and intimidating — a place enjoyed since 1665 by the Perceval lords of the manor — but this wonderful old house is now a place of faded glory and great charm. Sandy and Deb Perceval are as friendly and hospitable as can be. They take care of this estate with little help, doing most of the work themselves. Deb is responsible for the guest house and terraced gardens. Sandy farms half the 1000 acres, raising cattle and sheep. Fruit and vegetables are grown organically. The other half is in woodland and bog, where woodcock, snipe, and duck shoots are held in winter.

Two of the smaller sitting rooms, warmed by peat and log fires, are cozy lounges for guests' use. Furniture is a collection amassed over generations. Some bedrooms are so large that big round dining tables are casually placed as occasional tables to hold magazines and serve as writing desks. Most have canopied beds; all are well heated and have electric blankets.

Most Tuesday evenings offer a special treat. That's when Sandy goes into Sligo to join musicians who play Irish folk music to entertain themselves and their friends. He sings and plays the spoons and will take along any guests who want to go.

You can rent boats on Temple House Lake, well-known for its large and numerous pike, some of which weigh over 30 pounds. More than fifty varieties of birds have been seen on the estate in one day. Near the house is the ruin of a castle built in 1200.

We can't wait to return to this house, which has its roots so solidly in an aristocratic past but lives today in such a democratic present.

Price category: Moderate. *Proprietors:* Deb and Sandy Perceval. *Telephone:* (071) 83329. *Closed:* December through February. *Rooms:* 5, 2 with bath; private sitting room available. *Meals:* Dinner for guests; wine license. *Children:* Baby-sitting. *Facilities:* Sitting room, garden. *Activities:* Pike, perch, and bream fishing, boat rental, and shooting on the estate; ocean swimming, tennis, and riding nearby. *How to get there:* The house is easier to find from Route N17 than from Ballymote center. On Route N17, going north from Tobercurry, you will come to a long estate wall (Temple House estate) on your right, which will continue around a corner onto a side road. Follow the wall until you come to the third entrance, which has white gates and a gate house. Guests can be met at the Ballymote railway station.

BALLYNAHINCH CASTLE HOTEL

> O you who laboriously throw flies in English rivers,
> and catch . . . two or three feeble little brown trouts
> . . . how you would rejoice to have but an hour's sport
> in . . . Ballinahinch; where you have but to cast, and
> lo! a big trout springs at your fly, and after making
> a vain struggling, splashing, and plunging . . . is in-
> fallibly landed in the net.
> *William Makepeace Thackeray*, 1842

Thackeray arrived at Ballynahinch as a guest of the Martins, who had built the castle a century before. The most famous family member was Richard "Humanity Dick" Martin, founder of the Society for the Prevention of Cruelty to Animals in 1822. In 1927 the castle became the sporting lodge of His Highness, the Maharajah Jam Sahib of Nawanagan, better known as Ranjitsinhji, the famous cricketer. This wealthy Indian prince spent lavishly developing the famous fisheries that, as we know from Thackeray's words, were already remarkable. Those planning a fishing vacation should write for information and reserve a beat and a gillie. One reader who was not fishing but who enjoyed the atmosphere wrote, "The gillies are delivered each day from central casting. Special fishing place, but also great for walkers like me."

The castle's surroundings today must look much as Thackeray found them. The impression is of a wild confusion of beauty—flowering shrubs, wooded glens, green hillsides, melancholy mountains, and, over all, changing shadow and sunshine. Beneath a terrace the land drops steeply to a river where anglers with large salmon rods are casting, each wading in his own reserved beat, a gillie on the bank to help, if help should be needed, to gaff a fish.

The atmosphere is one of casual country-gentry elegance, with a rack for nets and rods in the front hall and large, comfortable chairs before crackling fires in elaborate Connemara marble fireplaces. Luncheon guests are likely to be in boots, either for fishing or for riding. On Satur-

day nights, hotel guests join many area patrons to listen to musicians play Irish music in the large public bar. Ballynahinch is a romantic outpost of past ages enhanced by the luxury of the twentieth century.

Price category: Moderate to expensive. *Manager:* John O'Connor. *Telephone:* (095) 31086. *Rooms:* 28 with bath and telephone. Christmas and New Year's programs. *Meals:* Breakfast, luncheon, snacks, dinner for public; full license. *Facilities:* Lounge, TV room, cocktail bar, public bar, garden. *Activities:* Lake and river fishing, woodcock shooting, tennis, at the hotel; ocean swimming, deep-sea fishing, and riding nearby. *U.S. agent:* RS. *How to get there:* The castle is signposted on Route N59, 41 miles west of Galway city. [T]

Ballyshannon, Donegal

DORRIAN'S IMPERIAL HOTEL

> . . . an odd, out-of-the-way little town ours, on the
> extreme western verge of Europe; our next neighbors,
> sunset way, being citizens of the great Republic. . . .
> *William Allingham,* 1864

In Allingham's little old town of Ballyshannon, there is a hotel on the main street which is patronized more by the Irish themselves than by tourists. It is not a country-house type of place, as are most of our recommendations. Established in 1781 and the center of town life ever since, it is probably the oldest hotel in Ireland still in its original building. We observed ladies meeting for lunch in the dining room, clerics greeting each other in the lobby, businessmen enjoying pub food in the bar. You might see a wedding reception or a gala twenty-first birthday party (the custom in Ireland is to celebrate a twenty-first birthday with an elaborate party similar to a wedding reception). Most of the furnishings are now modern, and Dorrian's, at first, has the feeling of a modern hotel. But there are antiques from earlier years in some public rooms.

The buildings of Ballyshannon are a picturesque jumble as they scramble up a hill. In one, a short walk from the hotel, is The Thatch, a pub owned by the Dorrian family. Furnished in old style, it's an inn where locals and visitors gather round an open fireplace to exchange conversation and where musical evenings and entertainment are frequent. If you'd like to absorb the life of an Irish town, try a night at Dorrian's Imperial Hotel.

Price category: Moderate. *Proprietors:* Benedict and Mary Dorrian. *Telephone:* (072) 51147. *Rooms:* 26 with bath, telephone, and TV. *Meals:* Luncheon, snacks, tea, dinner to the public; full license. *Children:* Baby-listening. *Facilities:* Lounge, cocktail bar, public bar. *Activities:* Indoor pool, ocean swimming, and boat rental nearby. *Credit cards:* Master, Visa. *How to get there:* Ballyshannon is on Route N15 between Sligo and Donegal. [T]

Ballyvaughan, Clare

GREGANS CASTLE HOTEL

The footprints of an elder race are here,
And memories of an old heroic time;
And shadows of an old mysterious faith
So that the place seems haunted and strange
    sounds float in the wind.

Anonymous

Near the edge of the Burren one rainy day, we entered the bar of Gregans Castle, a mock castle that was the seventeenth-century manor of the Martyn family. A splendid array of copper and brass hanging from beams and walls reflected the fire. We were smitten with the place, but it was the end of our trip, and we couldn't stay overnight. We've returned many times since, always eager to see what new luxuries Moira and Peter Haden have added.

Antique furniture and turf fires create an atmosphere of welcome and relaxation. Besides a full suite, there are some mini-suites — large bedrooms with a sitting room at one end and a dressing room leading to the bathroom. Golfers who stay here are less than a half hour away from the famous Lahinch golf links.

Only fresh produce is served. Fish from Galway Bay and local beef and lamb are beautifully presented in the attractive dining room. You can order lunch in the Corkscrew Bar, once the chapel, where you will find an unusual choice of snacks — soused herring, seafood quiche, smoked mackerel — as well as sandwiches and salads. On a good day, take lunch out to the terrace where Galway Bay sparkles in the distance and a sea of stone, the Burren, spreads out before your eyes.

The Burren — a weird, moonlike landscape of strange natural beauty that weaves a spell of mystery. Did it once echo with Druid chants? Who were the people who built these megalithic tombs and stone forts four thousand years ago? Why do streams plunge underground and small lakes disappear overnight? Why do these 100 square miles of rock garden display some of the rarest flowers on earth? The scenes are unlike any other in Ireland. No gorse or bracken carpets the hills, which rise in limestone terraces and slant down to the Atlantic. Plants from the Arctic intermingle with those from the Mediterranean; flowers far from their Alpine homes thrive beside native blooms. Ferns, lichens, and mosses cascade over stone, a soft green background for the riot of color that flourishes in rock crevices, in narrow clefts between the slabs, reaching its height in early summer. Botanists, geologists, and entomologists come to study; archaeologists and antiquarians come to roam the lonely heights and delve into puzzles of prehistory; spelunkers come to explore the miles of caves.

You will want to come back again — back to the Burren and back to Gregans Castle, which merits its reputation as one of Ireland's most popular small hotels. It is 37 miles from Shannon Airport and is our recommendation for your first night in Ireland if you are heading north.

Price category: Expensive to very expensive. *Proprietors:* Moira and Peter Haden. *Telephone:* (065) 77005. *Closed:* November through February. *Rooms:* 16 with bath; 3-day reduction; suitable for wheelchair guests. *Meals: Snacks, tea, and dinner for public; full license. Facilities:* Drawing room, lounge, TV room, public bar, garden. *Activities:* Ocean swimming, lake and deep-sea fishing, sailing, and surfing nearby. *Credit card:* Visa. *U.S. agent:* Robert Reid Associates. *How to get there:* The hotel is outside Ballyvaughan on Route N/69 to Lisdoonvarna. [T]

Ballyvaughan, Clare

HYLAND'S HOTEL

> The Burren . . . is one of the most extraordi-
> nary naturel phenomena in Ireland. . . . as far as
> the eye can see stretchs a stony wilderness . . .
> strangely wonderful and impressive.
>
> *Lynn Doyle,* 1936

In the picturesque village of Ballyvaughan on the shore of Galway Bay, this village-center hotel is managed by friendly Mary Hyland Green, the eighth generation of the Hyland family to carry on its good reputation. It is a nicer-than-average example of the village inn and a center of activities for the local people, plainly furnished with modern things. In the bar around its blazing turf fire, an impromptu musical session can start at any time, and the visitor is always welcome to join in.

When exploring the eerie Burren, which starts south from Ballyvaughan, we never miss a visit to the award-winning building that houses the Ailwee Cave. The architecture is fascinating, so cleverly designed to blend into the rock of the Burren that you don't see it at all until you are right upon it. Inside is a shop of fine Irish products and a tea room, as well as the entrance to the cave. Ballyvaughan itself has some nice craft shops.

Price category: Inexpensive. *Proprietor:* Mary Hyland Green. *Telephone:* (065) 77037. *Rooms:* 12, 9 with bath; all with telephone. *Meals:* Snacks, tea, dinner for public; full license. *Children:* Baby-sitting; playground. *Facilities:* Small hall lounge, TV room, public bar. *Activities:* Ocean swimming and deep-sea fishing nearby. *Credit cards:* Diners, Master, Visa. *U.S. agent:* RS. *How to get there:* Ballyvaughan is on Route N69 on Galway Bay.

BANSHA HOUSE

> It's a long, long way to Tipperary
> But my heart's right there.
>
> *Williams and Judge*

In the heart of Tipperary, which isn't really a long way from anywhere in Ireland, a warm country welcome awaits the traveler at Bansha House. A long avenue of beech trees leads to the imposing farmhouse set conveniently on the edge of the village.

There is nothing that smells quite like the fragrance of freshly baked bread, which was what greeted us here. Mary Marnane makes her own pastry and jam, too, and uses fresh produce from the farm to prepare hearty fare for the dining room. Big chintz-covered armchairs and sofa blend with Georgian arches and marble mantels typical of the period when Bansha House was built. It is carpeted throughout, and among the comfortable furnishings are a few antiques.

A road from Bansha leads to the secluded Glen of Aherlow, which spreads between the Galtee Mountains and the Slievenamuck hills and was once a refuge for dispossessed and outlawed Irish.

Price category: Very inexpensive. *Proprietor:* Mary Marnane. *Telephone:* (062) 54194. *Rooms:* 7, 4 with baths. *Meals:* Dinner for guests; no license. *Children:* Baby-sitting; playground. *Facilities:* Sitting room, garden. *Activities:* Riding and hunting nearby. *How to get there:* Bansha is 5 miles south of the town of Tipperary on Route N24.

CLONMEEN LODGE

With the sports of the field there's no pleasure can vie
While jocund we follow the hounds in full cry.
Paul Whitehead, 1734

The stamp of horses' hooves may wake you at Clonmeen Lodge, which is on a large estate that has bridle trails and a cross-country course. Lessons are given in all types of riding, from beginning to show jumping. Guests can also join the Duhallow Hunt.

Dagmar and Joerg Ott came from Germany. Dagmar, in charge of the house, loves to see her guests have a good time: She will arrange for them to play golf at reduced rates or to fish on the Blackwater for salmon and trout — she will even lend golf clubs and fishing gear. Nothing seems to be too much trouble.

The lodge's attractive lounge has an Oriental rug, some stripped pine antiques, a piano for guests to use, and a log fire. Bedrooms are of similar standard. The cocktail bar works on the honor system — write down on a card what you take. Seafood and fresh farm produce are prominent on a menu of both Irish and German specialties.

The Otts offer a package rate for a week of riding, picking up guests at the airport. Up to eight golfers can take the lodge for a week, be picked up and returned to the airport, and be driven to a different golf course each day. Write for further information on these.

The Lodge will pick up train travelers at Banteer. Guests can be driven for a day of sight-seeing in the area or can take a day trip by train to Cork city. With its ever-welcoming and friendly atmosphere, Clonmeen Lodge is a good stop for any traveler.

Price category: Inexpensive. *Proprietor:* Dagmar Ott. *Telephone:* (029) 56239. *Closed:* October and March. *Rooms:* 6 with bath. *Meals:* Dinner to public by reservation; full license. *Children:* Baby-sitting; ponies. *Facilities:* Sitting room, cocktail bar, garden. *Activities:* Riding, hunting, river swimming, trout and salmon fishing, and bicycle rental at the house. *Credit cards:* Diners, Master, Visa. *How to get there:* From Route R579 at Banteer, take a minor road that goes east, parallel with and just south of Route N72, the main Mallow to Killarney road. Clonmeen Lodge will be about 1 1/2 miles along on the right. Do not confuse it with Clonmeen House, which is on the same estate. Guests can be met at the Banteer train station.   [T]

BANTRY HOUSE

> The magnificent bay now glittered under the web of moonbeams which lay upon it; and I really thought myself in Paradise when I reached its shore.
> *Herman Ludwig Puckler-Muskay,* 1828

You can stay facing Bantry Bay, described above by a German prince, in a place that is very different from the usual hotel or bed-and-breakfast experience. Bantry House is a magnificent mansion, one of the great houses of Ireland open to the public for tours. Wings that once housed the kitchen and staff quarters have been remodeled into a tearoom, gift shop, bedrooms and sitting room for overnight guests.

The house was built about 1750 and added to over the years by the Earls of Bantry, ancestors of the present owner (who farmed for a time in Alabama). It is noted for its extravagant collection of antiques gathered in Ireland, Russia, Italy, Germany, France, and Belgium, mostly by the second earl in the early nineteenth century. Notable are Gobelin tapestries, seventeenth-century wainscoting of Spanish Cordovan leather, prints of Rome by Piranesi and Tiepolo, an Aubusson tapestry made for Marie Antoinette on her marriage, early Waterford chandelier and candelabra, and an eighteenth-century Savonnerie carpet. Family memorabilia include a coronet worn at the coronation of Queen Victoria and a letter written by Admiral Lord Nelson.

Overnight guests will find bedrooms pleasantly furnished in sunny light colors. Complimentary evening tea and cookies will be enjoyed in the old kitchen, now an attractive tearoom open to the public. They can roam the estate, with its formal gardens and splendid views, and those who stay for two nights will get a tour of the mansion.

Bantry House has won the Irish Tourist Board Award as Property of the Year. Although less personal than the usual bed-and-breakfast, it's a memorable place to stay.

Price category: Inexpensive to moderate. *Proprietors:* Egerton and Brigitte Shelswell-White. *Telephone:* (027) 50047. *Rooms:* 10, 8 with bath and telephone. *Meals:* Dinner by arrangement for guests; snacks and tea to public, 9 A.M. to 6 P.M. Wine license. *Facilities:* Sitting room, billiard room, and garden. *Activities:* Deep-sea fishing, boat trips, boat hire, scuba diving, water skiing, tennis nearby. *Credit cards:* Amex, Master, Visa. *How to get there:* Bantry House is on the main road.

THE GABLES

> There is a stone there
> That whoever kisses,
> Oh! he never misses
> To grow eloquent.
> *Francis Mahoney (Father Prout),* 1835

Famous Blarney Castle and its kissing stone are just a mile from this hundred-year-old house, which has a palm tree at its entrance and two acres of lawn, and gardens. The Gables was once the gift of the castle's owners to the local parish priest.

All is friendliness here, where the Lynch family will make you feel welcome right away. Their home is attractively decorated, and there's an easy graciousness about the place. We like the old woodwork that has been stripped of its former coats of paint, and we especially admired a Sheraton buffet in the dining room. Dinner is served upon advance request.

We enjoyed tea and scones before a fire later in the evening, with the Lynches and a friend of theirs who dropped in. If you are not sure whether or not you'd like staying in homes, the Gables would be an excellent one to try first.

Price category: Very inexpensive. *Proprietor:* Berna Lynch. *Telephone:* (021) 385330. *Closed:* November through February. *Rooms:* 4 with bath. *Meals:* Dinner for guests; no license. *Children:* Babysitting; reduction. *Facilities:* Living room, garden. *Activities:* Grass tennis court at the house; squash nearby. *Mailing address:* The Gables, Stoneview, Blarney, Cork. *How to get there:* The house is signposted in Blarney on the Cork road. After leaving the main road, drive more than a mile to the Gables, on the right.

Blessington, Wicklow

DOWNSHIRE HOUSE HOTEL

Wicklow . . . is the great delight of all Dublin residents, who are fortunate in having . . . at their doors . . . mountain, sea, wood, and river blended together in delicious landscapes . . . furnishing an environ that no other city in the world can boast.

John Murray, 1878

A country hotel, but not a "country-house" hotel, Downshire House has the atmosphere of a professional hostelry, but one where the guests are personally greeted by the resident owner and served by a friendly staff. As it is only 18 miles from Dublin, and in the middle of a village, it is a good spot for travelers who do not want to drive but would like some country living. Good bus service runs from the hotel's door into Dublin.

The hotel is not luxurious, but it is bright and comfortable. Lounges are pleasant, with paintings by local artists. Bedrooms are motel-like, smallish and neat, with individual thermostats. Ask for one at the back. The kitchen prepares fresh fish daily and bakes its own bread and cakes. Fresh butter, milk, eggs, poultry, and vegetables are delivered daily from neighboring farms.

The Blessington Sailing Club invites participation by hotel guests. Russborough House, right outside of town, is open to the public. Designed by Richard Castle, architect of Leinster House in Dublin (from which James Hoban drew inspiration when he designed the White House in Washington, D.C.), Russborough, with its 700-foot facade, has been called a perfect Georgian Palladian house. The plaster decorations on its walls are so elaborate they have been called "the ravings of a maniac." A superb art collection includes works by Vermeer, Rubens, Goya, and Gainsborough.

Price category: Inexpensive. *Proprietor:* Rhona Byrne. *Telephone:* (045) 65199. *Closed:* December 22 through January 12. *Rooms:* 25 with bath and telephone. *Meals:* Luncheon, snacks, tea, dinner for public; full license. *Children:* Baby-sitting; playground. *Facilities:* Lounge, TV lounge, garden. *Activities:* Tennis and game room at the hotel; riding, hang gliding, and free sailing nearby. *How to get there:* Blessington is on Route N81 south of Dublin.   [T]

TULFARRIS HOUSE HOTEL

Yes, this is Wicklow; round our feet
And o'er our heads its woodlands smile;
Behold it, love—the garden sweet
And playground of our stormy isle.
George Savage-Armstrong, 1892

We drove up a long tree-lined driveway that wends through the estate's sixty acres, passing fields where sheep graze. Manicured flower beds and Japanese cherry trees bloomed.

When we arrived in late morning, a fire in a marble fireplace warmed the drawing room, where swagged draperies of floral chintz in soft colors, pale Oriental rugs over wall-to-wall carpet, antique furniture, paintings, a crystal chandelier, and puffy chairs and sofas with lots of throw pillows gave the room a quality of serene elegance.

Decor in the Courtyard Bistro, where we had lunch, is surprising and clever. Such rustic elements as one wall all of stone, a display of horse brasses, and a fire blazing in a stone fireplace are mixed with white wicker furniture cushioned with flowered chintz. On warm days lunch can be served out in the courtyard, pleasant with the sound of water splashing in a fountain.

Deluxe bedrooms in the main section are distinguised with antiques, while standard rooms in a lower-ceilinged wing have good antique reproductions. All are large enough for sofas and chairs and overlook either the mountains behind or the lake in front of the house.

Recently opened, Tulfarris House should please the most particular. For those who want to take in the races, it's near the Curragh, Naas, and Punchestown.

Price category: Expensive to very expensive. *Proprietors:* Barry and Maureen Pocock. *Telephone:* (045) 64574. *Fax:* (045) 64423. *Rooms:* 21 with bath, telephone, and TV; 2 suites; suitable for wheel-chair guests; off-season breaks; Christmas and New Year programs. *Meals:* Luncheon, snacks, tea, dinner to public; full license. *Facilities:* Drawing room, cocktail lounge, terrace, garden, laundry service. *Activities:* Indoor pool, tennis, sauna, golf (9 holes), putting green, trout and pike fishing at hotel; lake swimming, water skiing, sailing, rowboat rental, and canal trip nearby. *Credit cards:* All. *U.S. agent:* RS. *How to get there:* Signposted on Route N81, 2 miles south of Blessington.   [T]

BALLYCORMAC HOUSE

> The dusky night rides down the sky,
> And ushers in the morn:
> The hounds all join in glorious cry,
> The huntsman winds his horn,
> And a-hunting we will go.
>
> *Henry Fielding,* 1733

Everyone is welcome at Ballycormac House, but those who like to be around horses will find this an exceptionally interesting place to stay. Hunting can be arranged with many packs, among them the Ormond and the Galway Blazers. The Paxmans will hunt with you and join you afterwards at the local pub to discuss the thrills of the chase.

Ballycormac House looks quite different from any other place we've stayed at in Ireland. An ancient small farm house, it is at least 400 years old. Decorating is of a sophisticated rustic style, with lots of old pine furniture, checked curtains, books, and cartoons of the hunt. Rooms are small and comfy; one sitting room has a raised fireplace, and all bedrooms have pine ceilings.

Rosetta is a Cordon Bleu cook, trained in London. She grows most of her own vegetables. All meals are enhanced by home-baked bread and homemade desserts.

Ballycormac House is in secluded green countryside. Railed paddocks and fields and stabling for the Paxmans' own hunters are behind the house. John conducts a week of trail riding every other week from mid-May to mid-September. (Send for a brochure if interested.) But remember, Ballycormac is not just for the horsey set. It makes an attractive and very inexpensive overnight.

Price category: Very inexpensive. *Proprietors:* John and Rosetta Paxman. *Telephone:* (067) 21129. *Rooms:* 4 with bath; 1 suite. *Meals:* Dinner for guests; wine license. *Children:* Baby-sitting. *Facilities:* Sitting room, TV room, garden. *Activities:* Riding at house; boat trips on Lough Derg, row-boat and outboard rentals, and sailing nearby. *Mailing address:* Ballycormac, Aglish, Borrisokane, Tipperary. *How to get there:* From Borrisokane, take the first right turn north of the village. Continue to the end and turn left. Find signs for Ballycormac House.

Bruckless, Donegal

BRUCKLESS HOUSE

> Donegal gives an insatiable feeling of romantic remoteness, where whispering grasses blend in a pastoral of greens.
>
> *Jill Uris, 1980*

Serene and secluded, Bruckless House is on 19 leafy acres that border a bay. The solid stone house was built in 1738 by a Mr. Cassidy, who made money in sailing ships, including transporting slaves to the United States. Large trees on the property were grown from sequoia seeds brought back from the Muir Woods of California.

In the entrance hall, with a grandfather clock, the flagstone floor is warmed by Oriental rugs. A large living room, where chairs with flowered slipcovers are grouped before a log fire, is a gracious setting for evening conversation with other guests. Bedrooms are plain, and some are small.

The interesting owners lived in Hong Kong, where Clive was with the police force. He is Welsh but has learned a great deal about the history of this area and enjoys chatting with his guests. Joan is Irish. They breed Connemara ponies and Irish draft horses. The latter are bred to thoroughbreds to produce the finest hunters and show jumpers.

This is a good place for those traveling alone: Two of the bedrooms are singles, and everyone is friendly.

Price category: Very inexpensive. *Proprietors:* Clive and Joan Evans. *Telephone:* (073) 3707. *Closed:* October through March. *Rooms:* 5, 1 with bath; 2 2-bedroom self-catering cottages. *Meals:* Dinner for guests; no license. *Facilities:* Living room, garden. *Activities:* Ocean swimming at house. Deep-sea river and lake fishing and riding nearby. *How to get there:* The house is on Route N56 as you come to Bruckless, about 12 miles west of Donegal town. Drive through the entrance gates, follow signs to the house, and open gates you come to if they are closed. Close gates behind you.

COOLEEN HOUSE

> A genial hearth, a hospitable board, and a refined rusticity.
>
> *William Wordsworth,* 1793

This agreeable farmhouse lodging was built for a bishop 320 years ago. When we arrived, a fire was going behind an old fire fender in an inviting sitting-dining room. The sheen of polished silver on an antique dumbwaiter, the tapestry-covered chairs drawn up around the fireplace, and velvet draperies gave the room a warm and welcoming appearance. The bedrooms are large but lack central heating—no drawback during the months the house takes guests except during an unseasonable nippy spell.

Soft-spoken Eileen McDonagh takes a personal interest in the comfort of her guests. She will serve dinner each evening if she knows in time that you will be there for it. Guests sit together at two mahogany tables.

Pedigreed Friesian cattle are raised on the 100-acre farm that overlooks the River Maigue. You can try your luck for salmon or trout in it; fishing gear can be rented in town if you haven't brought your own. The bishop's old church on the farm is no longer used for services, but you can wander through its ancient graveyard. Those who enjoy farmhouse lodgings will find Cooleen House most appealing.

Price category: Very inexpensive. *Proprietor:* Eileen McDonagh. *Telephone:* (063) 90584. *Closed:* October through April. *Rooms:* 4 with shared baths. *Meals:* Dinner for guests; no license. *Children:* Baby-sitting. *Facilities:* Sitting room, garden. *Activities:* Salmon and trout fishing and river swimming at the house; tennis and riding nearby. *How to get there:* Cooleen House is signposted on the Limerick–Cork road, Route N20.   [T]

ASHLING

My garden is a pleasant place
Of sun glory and leaf grace,
O Friend, wherever you may be,
Will you not come to visit me?

Louise Driscoll, 1927

Lucky are they who stay in this house by the side of the road. As soon as they turn into the driveway, they'll see that it is exceptionally well cared for. Its lovely gardens have won the national award for the best garden among the town and country homes that take guests.

Although Ashling is a modern one-story house, there are many antiques scattered among the attractive furnishings. Fires of peat and logs burn under a Victorian overmantle. Guests dine together on an antique dining table surrounmded by period chairs. Three grandfather clocks tick the hours. Floor-to-ceiling windows in one lounge look across the garden to the Galtee mountains. You'll be warm in any weather in beds equipped with electric blankets.

Hospitality here is warm and gracious. Ashling is a pleasure to stay in besides being conveniently placed to visit the Rock of Cashel.

Price category: Very inexpensive. *Proprietor:* Mrs Breda Fitzgerald. *Telephone:* (052) 41601. *Rooms:* 3 with bath; ground-floor rooms. *Meals:* Dinner for guests; wine license. *Children:* Baby-sitting. *Facilities:* Sitting room, TV lounge, garden. *How to get there:* Ashling is less than a mile outside Cahir on the Dublin Road.

KILCORAN LODGE HOTEL

Were you ever in sweet Tipperary
Where the fields are so sunny and green,
And the heath-brown Slievebloom and the Galtees
Look down with so proud a mien.
Eva Kelly, 1855

In the Golden Vale of Tipperary, shifting colors of green and heather on the foothills become misty shadows of blue and purple on the distant mountains encircling Kilcoran Lodge.

A cozy lobby–lounge with a grouping of bamboo-look chairs before a Victorian fireplace welcomes guests. Snare room 20, if you can; it is the only bedroom furnished with antiques — large carved writing desk, cheval mirror, Victorian chairs, armoire — and it has a grand view. Other bedrooms are nicely decorated with modern furniture and pleasant color schemes. Some have balconies and overlook rose gardens. Have an Irish coffee on the terrace as we did, enjoying the Irish twilight. At ten o'clock we could still see the Knockmealdown Mountains way to the south. The menu included fresh seafood, good steak, lamb and veal, interesting vegetable dishes, and a well-chosen wine list.

Kilcoran Lodge is deep in hunting country, and you can follow the hounds with such famous packs as the South Tipperary Foxhounds, Black and Tan Beagles, or Clonmel Harriers. If you enjoy fishing, an expert ghillie will lead you to the best beats for trout or salmon.

This hotel is a convenient overnight stop between southwest Ireland and Dublin.

Price category: Moderate. *Manager:* George Haines. *Telephone:* (052) 41288. *Rooms:* 30 with bath, telephone, tea-making, and TV; Christmas program. *Meals:* Luncheon, snacks, tea, dinner for public; full license. *Children:* Baby-sitting and -listening. *Facilities:* Lobby–lounge, cocktail bar, garden. *Activities:* Sauna, exercise room, and indoor pool at the lodge; salmon and trout fishing, riding, and hunting nearby. *How to get there:* The lodge is 5 miles south of Cahir on the Fermoy Road. [T]

RICHMOND HOUSE

> . . . parks and rocks covered with the grandest foliage;
> rich handsome seats of gentlemen in the midst of fair
> lawns and beautiful bright plantations and shrubberies.
> *William Makepeace Thackeray,* 1842

Richmond House was one of the handsome seats of gentlemen
Thackeray was describing in his tour of this section of Ireland. A long
driveway leads past cattle in fields to an imposing 300-year-old mansion where Jean Deevy will welcome you. At this relaxed and friendly
guesthouse, antiques of many periods harmonize with the old building.
Among them are a grandfather clock, large gilt-framed mirrors, and
Oriental rugs, complementing velvet and cretonne-covered chairs and
marble mantels. Books are in tall mahogany cases. Dinner is served
every evening; if you arrive too late for it, Jean says she'll always fix
something for you.

Be sure to drive from here over the spectacular Vee Road to Tipperary. On the way, you can tour the gardens of the Duke of Devonshire's Lismore Castle, which was a home of the former Adele Astaire.
The Ring, an Irish-speaking area, is nearby, as are sandy beaches.

Price category: Very inexpensive. *Proprietors:* Jean and Bill Deevy.
Telephone: (058) 54278. *Closed:* October 31 through February 1.
Rooms: 9, 5 with bath. *Meals:* Dinner for public by reservation; wine
license. *Children:* Baby-sitting. *Facilities:* Lounge, garden. *Activities:*
Riding and sea fishing nearby. *How to get there:* The house is a half
mile from Cappoquin on the road to Dungarvan.   [T]

Carlingford, Louth

VIEWPOINT

> I'll wait for the wild rose that's waitin' for me,
> Where the Mountains of Mourne sweep down to
> the sea.
>
> *Percy French,* 1899

Floor to ceiling windows of Viewpoint offer superb views across Carlingford Bay to the Mountains of Mourne sweeping down to the sea. This home of modern design nestles into a heather-covered hillside on the Cooley peninsula. Here Paul and Marie Woods offer warm and gracious hospitality. Paul, who owns a manufacturing business, is an avid gardener. Luxuriant plants and flowers thrive inside and out.

Marie has decorated the house with flair in strong colors. Five unusually large bedrooms, comfortable with couches and chairs, are downstairs at a garden level, as the house is on a slope. The bedroom on the entrance level is rather small. The Woods have had so many repeat guests, and guests referred by guests, that they have added six bedrooms, each with a separate entrance, in a new building beside the house.

A terrace surrounded by colorful blooms is a lovely spot from which to watch cruisers and sailboats on the bay. There's a grill on it that guests are invited to use. Many like to buy food in the village to cook dinner outdoors on a beautiful evening. The Woods don't serve dinner and have no license, but McKevitt's Village Inn is nearby.

The picturesque Cooley peninsula has a rugged beauty. Known as Cuchulain Country, this was the demesne of Ireland's most celebrated warrior of ancient sagas. King John's Castle, a large fortification on a rock overlooking Carlingford harbour, has a gateway noted for having been designed to admit only a single horseman at a time. This beautiful, historic area is far off the usual American tourist route.

Price category: Very inexpensive. *Proprietors:* Maria and Paul Woods. *Telephone:* (042) 73149. *Rooms:* 11 with bath, TV, and tea-making. *Children:* Baby-sitting. *Facilities:* Living room, laundry, garden. *Activities:* Ocean swimming, windsurfing, sailing, and tennis nearby. *How to get there:* From Dundalk, start north on Route N1. Turn right onto Route R173 and find Viewpoint just north of Carlingford.

Carrick-on-Shannon, Roscommon

GLENCARNE HOUSE

If you would like to see the height of hospitality,
The cream of kindly welcome, and the core of cordiality.
Francis A. Fahy

You could hardly find a friendlier place to stay in Ireland than with the Harrington family at Glencarne House. Their eighteenth-century Georgian farmhouse, set amid trees, flowering shrubs, and bright flowers, is an attractive sight as you approach up a long curving drive. The decor inside the house is homey, with many good antiques scattered about, including an inlaid piano waiting for a guest to play it. Guests eat together at a large oaken dining table before a tile-faced hearth with a brass fender. Food, most of it from the farm, is outstandingly good and plentiful.

At Lough Key Forest Park, only half a mile from Glencarne House, you can walk along nature trails and see deer in an enclosure, or visit a bog garden with varieties of rhododendron and heather and other bog-loving plants. A restaurant and gift shop are beside the water, and take-out food may be enjoyed at picnic tables. The Harringtons keep a boat with outboard for guests to use on the island-dotted lake, where you can also take a launch trip with commentary.

Glencarne House has been a national winner as the best farmhouse lodging. The Harringtons like Americans and get many repeat guests. One American visitor has gone back every year for more than ten years.

Price category: Very inexpensive. *Proprietors:* Agnes and Pat Harrington. *Telephone:* (079) 67013. *Closed:* October through February. *Rooms:* 6, 3 with bath. *Meals:* Dinner for guests; no license. *Children:* Baby-sitting. *Facilities:* Living room, garden. *Activities:* Lake swimming, outdoor pool, boat rental, boat trips, tennis, riding, and trout, bream, and pike fishing nearby. *Mailing address:* Glencarne House, Ardcarne, Carrick-on-Shannon, County Roscommon. *How to get there:* The house is on Route N4 between Carrick-on-Shannon and Boyle. [T]

CEDARFIELD HOUSE

Among the meadows of the countryside,
From city noise and tumult far away.
John Russell Hayes

Cedarfield House seems to be far in the countryside, but its long tree-lined driveway is right off the main route across southern Ireland. Very beautiful, mature, chestnut trees and rhododendron frame the recently refurbished house. A simply-decorated living room is cheerful with a log fire. Bedrooms are pleasant, the largest being on the third floor.

You can count on the quality of the food: Tom Hatton's cooking draws many from the neighborhood. Dinner started with a choice of mushroom croustades, cheese soufflé, or paupiettes of rainbow trout with leeks on cavier sauce. Vegetable soup came next, followed by filet mignon, veal with mushrooms and mustard sauce, lamb cutlet, or sole and salmon roulade. After several dessert choices, coffee or tea with petit fours finished the bountiful meal.

Near Carrick-on-Suir is the recently-established Tipperary Crystal, staffed by former Waterford Glass skilled master craftsmen. You can watch them at work and make purchases in the factory shop. Cedarfield House is a convenient, easy-to-find stopover for those driving west after arriving in Rosslare on the ferry from Britain.

Price category: Inexpensive. *Proprietors:* Anne and Tom Hatton. *Telephone:* (051) 40164. *Rooms:* 5 with bath, telephone, and TV. *Meals:* Dinner for guests daily, for public Monday through Saturday; wine license. *Facilities:* Living room, garden. *Activities:* Riding, tennis, and fishing nearby. *How to get there:* Cedarfield House Is on Route N24, just east of Carrick-on-Suir.

Cashel Bay, Galway

CASHEL HOUSE

> One of the most wild and beautiful districts that it
> is ever the fortune of the traveller to examine.
> *William Makepeace Thackeray*, 1842

Try to get into Cashel House, for it is certainly one of the best country-house hotels in Ireland. Nothing beats a hotel well run by its owners. Dermot McEvilly's baliwick is the kitchen, where he is the master chef, ordering, marketing, and overseeing the cooking, most of which he does himself. Kay is in charge at the front. In the dining room she comes to each table to greet her guests and ask, "Would you like a bit more salmon? Another cutlet?" Son Frank has joined the team. He'll tell you about the history of Connemara and help you plan your days' outings.

This former private manor, on the road that Thackeray described between Galway and Clifden, was owned by a botanist who brought plants from all over the world, including Tibet. When General Charles De Gaulle and his wife stayed at Cashel House for two weeks of their Irish holiday in 1969, he spent many hours on the wooded walks that meander through the estate. The azalea walk is magnificent in spring. If you can't stay overnight, stop in for a snack lunch in the bar. Its large windows look out over a colorful Irish country garden.

Many German and French guests come to Cashel House to fish. Every evening, trout wrapped in clear plastic are displayed in the hall. Each is marked with its weight and the name of the fisherman who caught it. The next morning the hall is lined with wicker hampers holding picnic lunches. Even if you don't intend to fish, order a hamper for a picnic one day. Take it, perhaps, to Connemara's isolated southwest corner, where blue turf-smoke hangs over lonely thatched cottages, and only the cry of the seagull and the crash of waves disturbs the silent white beaches. The hotel has its own equestrian center where you can take lessons from a qualified instructor or join a group for trail riding.

Cashel House is one of the few Irish members of the Relais et Chateaux group of prestigious, privately owned hotels, with headquarters in France. It is the epitome of all that is best in country inns.

Price category: Expensive. *Proprietors:* Dermot and Kay McEvilly. *Telephone:* (095) 31001. *Closed:* November to mid-March. *Rooms:* 30 with bath; suitable for wheelchair guests. *Meals:* Luncheon, snacks, tea, dinner for public; full license. *Children:* Not suitable for those under six. *Facilities:* Drawing room, TV room, library, cocktail lounge, garden. *Activities:* Ocean swimming, riding, tennis, and sail- and rowboats at the hotel; deep-sea fishing nearby. *Credit cards:* Amex, Master, Visa. *U.S. agent:* Selective Hotels. *How to get there:* The hotel is on the coast on a minor road south of Route N59, between Recess and Clifden. [T]

ZETLAND HOTEL

Wild and wide as the prospect around us is, it has somehow a kindly, friendly look.
William Makepeace Thackeray, 1842

Lovely Zetland Hotel, overlooking Cashel Bay, is decorated in a pleasing, uncluttered manner. The inviting interiors are warm and fragrant
with the scent of turf fires; watercolors depict the otherworldly Connemara landscape.

Edward VII and Queen Alexandra once stayed here, and you can
slumber in the Red Suite, where they slept. The bedrooms are furnished
with antiques and traditional reproductions. We like best the rooms
facing the sea that have bathrooms with radiant-heated floors of green
Connemara marble. The presidents of West Germany and Ireland have
been guests.

The Zetland has two popular bars: the comfortable Lounge Bar,
where hot and cold snacks are available, a good lunch stop if you are
driving through the area; and the convivial Public Bar, where traditional music is sometimes heard. The latter has its own entrance and
is patronized by local people.

Known to generations of fishermen, the Zetland offers some of the best fishing in Ireland, with boats and gillies available. Excellent sea fishing, both inshore and deep-sea, can be had locally.

Price category: Expensive to very expensive. *Proprietors:* John and Mona Prendergast. *Telephone:* (095) 31111. *Closed:* November to mid-March. *Rooms:* 20 with bath. *Meals:* Luncheon, snacks, tea, dinner for public; full license. *Facilities:* Lounge, TV room, cocktail bar, public bar, garden. *Activities:* Salmon and deep-sea fishing, ocean swimming, and riding nearby. *Credit cards:* Amex, Master, Visa. *U.S. agent:* RS. *How to get there:* The hotel is on a minor road south of Route N59 between Recess and Clifden. Guests can be met at the Shannon or Galway airports. [T]

Cashel, Tipperary

CASHEL PALACE HOTEL

Cashel of the Kings,
What memories it brings!
Its tradition sings
So sweetly to the heart.

Anonymous

From the windows of the Cashel Palace Hotel there is an unparalleled view of the Rock of Cashel rising out of the surrounding plain, beautiful in the sunlight but magnificent when floodlighted at night. These ecclesiastical ruins are to Ireland what the Acropolis is to Greece. In the middle of the fifth century Saint Patrick converted Irish King Aengus to Christianity here, and in 1002 Brian Boru was crowned ''king of all Ireland.'' Among the ruins is a thirteenth-century cathedral burned in

1495 by the earl of Kildare, who explained to King Henry VII of England that he burned it because he thought his enemy, Archbishop Creagh, was inside. During the tumultuous sixteenth century, Queen Elizabeth I had the archbishop of Cashel executed without trial.

Cashel Palace was designed for a later archbishop by the great Palladian architect Sir Edward Pearce, who designed Parliament House in Dublin, now the Bank of Ireland. The palace was built in 1730 and is a perfect example of Queen Anne architecture. From the enormous drawing room with 18-foot ceilings, French doors lead to gardens where you can sit and have tea under the shadow of the Rock. The formal dining room is next to it, and another is in the vaulted cellar. A taproom is a favorite meeting place for local people, who gather before lunch or in the evening. Walls are resplendent with large oil paintings of magnificent Irish thoroughbreds as well as watercolors, engravings, and Irish hunting prints of the nineteenth century. One of the bathrooms has murals of playful rabbits, painted by a bishop for his child.

This luxurious hotel is known for its fine food. It is right in the center of the small town, a nice spot from which to browse around in shops and see local life.

Price category: Very expensive. *Proprietor:* Ray Carroll. *Telephone:* (062) 61411. *Rooms:* 20 with bath and telephone; suites and ground-floor rooms. *Meals:* Breakfast, luncheon, snacks, tea, dinner for public; full license. *Children:* Baby-sitting. *Facilities:* Drawing room, lounge, public bar, garden. *Activities:* Trout and salmon fishing, riding, and hunting nearby. *Credit cards:* Amex, Diners, Master, Visa. *U.S. agent:* Robert Reid Associates. *How to get there:* The hotel is in the center of Cashel, which is on Route N8.   [T]

DOYLE'S SCHOOLHOUSE

> All human history attests
> That happiness for man, — the hungry sinner! —
> Since Eve ate apples, much depends on dinner.
> *Lord Byron,* 1818

If dining well while traveling is among your priorities, a stay at Doyle's Schoolhouse will fill the bill. Although best known for its restaurant, the old schoolhouse offers bedrooms, not large but decorated in pretty colors and soft prints. The largest has an antique desk and sleigh bed. Continental quilts cover the beds, but you can have sheets and blankets if you ask in time. Bathrooms have showers.

A friendly welcome from John Doyle sets the tone for a delightful evening. Turf and log fires burn under marble mantels in two attractive lounges, one reserved for house guests, the other for both house and dinner guests. Furnishings are an eclectic mix of good old pieces. John knows antiques and even deals a bit. One modern note is a steep spiral iron stairway to some of the bedrooms, not suitable for anyone who has any difficulty with stairs.

A proprietor-chef like John Doyle is dedicated to turning out consistantly fine food. His superb meals, while not inexpensive like the bedrooms, are good value and entice people from as far as Dublin, an hour away. You can count on everything being freshly prepared. The wine list, too, is well chosen.

Castledermot is a place of historical interest. Many come to see its Celtic high crosses, Norman arch, ancient round tower, carved Viking stone, and the remains of a Franciscan monastery. Be sure to visit the National Stud and Japanese Gardens, which are on the same grounds in nearby Kildare.

Price category: Inexpensive. *Proprietor:* John Doyle. *Telephone:* (0503) 44282. *Rooms:* 8 with bath and tea-making. *Meals:* Dinner for public except Sunday and Monday, November through March (dinner for guests by arrangement on those evenings); wine license. *Children:* Not suitable. *Facilities:* Living room, lounge, garden. *Activities:* Riding and tennis nearby. *Credit cards:* Amex, Master, Visa. *How to get there:* Castledermot is on Route N9, about midway between Athy and Carlow.

KILKEA CASTLE

Strange scenes have pass'd within thy walls, and
    strange
Has been thy fate through many a chance and
    change!
Thy towers have heard the war-cry, and the shout
Of friends within, and answering foe without,
Have rung to sounds of revelry, while mirth
Held her carousal. . . .

James Bird

New owners have recently refurbished and reopened Kilkea Castle, which has been standing for eight centuries, watching the ebb and flow of history through its medieval windows. It was one of the earliest Norman castles built in Ireland and one of the very few that has been lived in continuously ever since.

For centuries the pattern of life was of intermittent war. For most of this time the castle belonged to the Fitzgeralds, earls of Kildare, the most powerful famiy in Ireland. At times they gave only a devious loyalty to the English king, preferring to be left in peace to make their own wars. In Tudor times, Gerald Fitzgerald, known as the Wizard Earl, changed his religion three or four times, swaying with the winds of power to protect his estates.

The widow of one of his successor earls gave Kilkea to the Jesuit order, which used it for twelve years in one of the few times the castle left Fitzgerald control. After the Restoration, the family regained Kilkea but let it out on lease for two hundred years. The castle went downhill under successive tenants.

In the famine years of the nineteenth century, the Fitzgerald owner, by now Duke of Leinster and resident at palatial Carton House, decided to convert the medieval castle into a family residence with all the comforts of Victorian days. Unlike many of the landlords, he seems to have spent his substantial revenues where they were produced, for restoring Kilkea was one of the "make-work" projects he embarked upon to give local employment. Once again it became a family home, perhaps the dower house for a widowed duchess, a luxurious pad for a grown son, or a refuge for other family members needing a place to live.

The family gradually fell upon difficult financial times. Carton House was sold, but some Fitzgeralds hung on at Kilkea Castle until

1960. The last one, Lord Walter, earned respect as one of Ireland's foremost antiquarian scholars. He liked to converse in Irish and used English with a strong Irish accent until he became excited, when he would revert to the upper-class English accent of his education.

Crystal chandeliers and candlelight provide illumination in the dining room, once the great hall where wandering Irish bards provided entertainment in return for food and a warm fire. Antique furniture predominates. Bedrooms are decorated with floral fabrics and have such extras as video and hair dryers; those in the castle are more expensive than the ones off the courtyard.

Guests often enjoy the evening in a rustic taproom, where patrons sometimes break out in song. If you want just a short trip into the past, stop at Kilkea Castle for a pub lunch. You may eat on a terrace outside the bar while admiring the gardens. Kilkea is a fascinating link with ancient times.

Price category: Moderate to very expensive. *Manager:* Shane Cassidy. *Telephone:* (0503) 45156. *Closed:* Christmas. *Rooms:* 43 with bath, telephone, and TV; 3 suites. *Meals:* Bar snacks and dinner for public; full license. *Children:* Baby-sitting and -listening. *Facilities:* 2 lounges, cocktail bar, public bar, garden. *Activities:* Indoor pool, tennis, clay-pigeon shooting at the castle; riding nearby. *Credit cards:* Amex, Diners, Master, Visa. *How to get there:* The castle is 3 miles northwest of Castledermot on the Athy road.   [T]

AISLING

> One wonders in these places why anyone is left in Dub-
> lin, or London, or Paris, when it would be better, one
> would think, to live in a tent . . . with this magnificent
> sea and sky, and to breathe this wonderful air.
> *John Millington Synge,* 1907

Synge was visiting the beautiful Dingle peninsula when he wrote the
words above, but you won't need a tent if you stay at Aisling (pronounced "Ashling"), a fine bed-and-breakfast home in one of the peninsula's little towns.

The tastefully decorated rooms in this modern house reflect the character of the hostess. In the living room some antique cabinets and
tables — on one a chess board is ready for play — stand on parquet floors.
Attractive upholstered pieces, pleasing dried-flower arrangements, and
many books add to the serene atmosphere of this room, where guests
are soon enjoying each other's company. Helen Healy is knowledgeable about the culture and history of Ireland since ancient times and
speaks fluent Irish. All visitors give Aisling high marks.

On a clear day take Conor Pass, the road that switchbacks over the
mountains to Dingle. The scenery is spectacular. Have lunch at Doyle's
Seafood Bar, which earned a listing in Michelin and won a National
Barfood Competition. Return over the Slieve Mish mountains by way
of the Camp road, going through Annascaul, where the South Pole Inn
recalls Antarctic exploration. Thomas Crean left from here to join Captain Robert Scott's expedition; it was he who found Scott and his
companions in their tent after their fatal return from the South Pole.

Aisling's loyal guests keep it well filled; it's a place people enjoy staying for a few days. Mrs. Healy will recommend restaurants.

Price category: Very inexpensive. *Proprietor:* Helen Healy. *Telephone:* (066) 39134. *Closed:* October through April. *Rooms:* 6, 2 with
bath; ground-floor rooms. *Children:* Baby-sitting. *Facilities:* Lounge,
TV lounge, garden. *Activities:* Ocean swimming nearby. *How to get
there:* Start west from Tralee on Route R559. From Camp take a minor
road to Castlegregory.

Castlelyons, Cork

BALLYVOLANE HOUSE

> Who can tell the pleasures of fancy when fancy takes
> her ease in an old country-house, while the twilight
> darkens the corners of expressive rooms, and the ap-
> preciative intruder, pausing at the window, sees the
> great soft billows of the lawn melt away into the park?
> *Henry James,* 1877

Among the delights of Ballyvolane are the trees — especially the copper beech. Golden splashes of daffodils everywhere caught our eye in
May. Glorious flowering shrubs abound, and bluebells carpet the woods
in the parkland. The old-world charm of the outside is complemented
by a mixture of elegance and coziness within. All rooms in this old family home put treasures to daily use.

When Jeremy and Merrie Green decided to take paying guests to help support the upkeep of Ballyvolane, they wanted to provide the kind of atmosphere friends create for friends. Neighbors are sometimes invited to join guests for dinner in the large candlelit dining room. A log fire blazes here in cool weather. Friendly conversation continues over after-dinner coffee and drinks in a sitting room, where two cairn terriers and a spaniel are likely to be dozing on the Oriental rugs.

The charming bedrooms, decorated in pretty colors, have big wardrobes instead of closets. One bathroom has a wonderful old tub encased in mahogany, with mahogany steps to help you in.

The Greens will arrange for guests to play tennis on either a friend's court or at a local club, or to fish for salmon and trout on the Blackwater River.

Price category: Moderate. *Proprietors:* Jeremy and Merrie Green. *Telephone:* (025) 36349. *Rooms:* 5, 3 with bath; 1 ground floor room; self-catering apartment. *Meals:* Dinner for guests. *Children:* Babysitting, toys. *Facilities:* Sitting room, game room, garden. *Activities:* Salmon and trout fishing, tennis, riding, hunting, clay pigeon shooting, indoor pool nearby. *How to get there:* Take Route N8 from Fermoy. A few miles along, see Castlelyons posted on the left. Ask in the village for Ballyvolane House.   [T]

CLONALIS HOUSE

> Clonalis of the muted wood, the incense-fragrant cypress,
> Still house, where O'Carolon's harp stands silent.
> Memories here are gathered thick as yellowing leaves
> Of Ireland's sad seasons, generations
> Who kept the faith with the High King of an inner
> kingdom.
>
> *Kathleen Raine,* 1973

Clonalis House, ancestral home of the O'Connors of Connaught, whose forebears were high kings of Ireland, is a repository of history. Unique among the great houses of Ireland, it celebrates a Gaelic-Irish tradition rather than an Anglo-Irish one.

In 1186, King Rory O'Conor, whose ancestors were kings of Connaught since the fourth century, had to surrender his territory to the Norman invaders, but over the centuries the O'Conors have retrieved 700 acres. The present resident, Pyers O'Conor-Nash, was a barrister in Dublin before he inherited the estate. To ensure its preservation and share its history, he opens the house to the public daily in July and August and on weekends in May and June. From November through January, shooting parties of from four to eight people come to hunt duck, pheasant, snipe, and woodcock.

Pyers and Marguerite, his wife, are a charming young couple who will make you feel most welcome. They have children and will gladly accept yours. They dine with their guests and spend time with them later. Conversation tends to return to the history of Clonalis and the O'Conors, an embodiment of the history of Ireland itself. The house goes back only to 1878, and the O'Conor who built it would still feel quite at home, except for the modernized bathrooms and kitchen and good central heat. The four guest bedrooms all have half-tester double beds.

Many rooms of the mansion are set up to display historic objects. In one is an exhibit of clothing worn by members of the family from about 1700. In another, the harp of O'Carolan, most famous of the old Irish bards who provided entertainment in return for hospitality, takes center stage. There's a priceless collection of archival material on parchment, vellum, and paper, such as the last recorded verdicts under the old Brehon law and records of 60 generations of O'Conors. Letters from such celebrities as Anthony Trollope, Daniel O'Connell, and Douglas Hyde are shown.

Those who love history should make a real effort to stay at Clonalis House.

Price category: Moderate. *Proprietors:* Pyers and Marguerite O'Conor-Nash. *Telephone:* (0907) 20014. *Closed:* November through April. *Rooms:* 4, 2 with bath. *Meals:* Dinner for guests; tea for public when house is open to tour. *Children:* Baby-sitting. *Facilities:* Drawing room, library, garden. *Activities:* Grass tennis court at the house; outdoor pool and rowboat rental nearby. *Mailing address of agent:* Elegant Ireland, 15 Harcourt Street, Dublin 2. *How to get there:* The house is a half mile from Castlerea on the road to Castlebar, Route N60. Overnight guests can be met at the Castlerea train station.   [T]

Castletownsend, Cork

BOW HALL

> The huge shoulder of the headland is beautiful with
> heather . . . the pink sea-thrift meets the heather at
> the verge of the cliffs . . . the fuchsia bushes have fed
> on the Food of the Gods and have become trees.
> *Edith Somerville,* 1887

This seventeenth-century Queen Anne house is now home to Barbara
and Dick Vickery from midwestern America. They first saw Ireland
in 1970; conquered by its charms, they returned yearly, staying in guest
houses and making friends up and down the west coast. They began
to dream of a new life. Their children were grown; wouldn't it be fun
to move to Ireland and open a guest house of their own! So here they

are, serving American food to Irish and English guests. Would pancakes and hot muffins go over for breakfast, or would the Irish want their familiar "fry" — bacon, eggs, and soda bread? The Irish loved pancakes. Staying with the Vickerys, they experienced a bit of American culture. One English couple who chanced upon Bow Hall in September returned for Christmas.

To Barbara, cooking is an art. She makes everything from scratch, even grinding her own wheat berries for yeast breads. Dick is a super gardener. The tiered garden that falls away below the house supplies most of the vegetables for the table. A typical dinner might start with vegetable soup and be followed by freshly-caught salmon, parsley buttered new potatoes, a garden vegetable, and always a tossed green salad, so seldom found in Ireland or Britain. Meat or poultry is available for those who prefer it. Crusty homemade bread is always on the table, and for dessert Barbara makes a cake, tart, or pudding and features home-made ice cream.

The Vickerys shipped over all their own furniture, most of it antique. One end of the living room is a library where guests love to browse, then snuggle up before one of the flickering fireplaces and read to a background of stereo music. Dick's walled garden provides a profusion of flowers for Barbara to arrange throughout the home. All bedrooms but one overlook the harbor described in the quotation above.

Castletownsend is one of Ireland's prettiest little towns. Edith Somerville described its life in her nineteenth-century books, written with her cousin, using the pen name of Somerville and Ross. Edith knew Bow Hall; it was then home to Admiral Somerville, a relative. Talking with the Vickerys about the differences between life in Ireland and life in the United States is fascinating.

Price category: Moderate. *Proprietors:* Barbara and Dick Vickery. *Telephone:* (028) 36114. *Closed:* December. *Rooms:* 3 with bath. 3-day reduction. *Meals:* Dinner for public by reservation; no license. *Facilities:* Living room–library, garden. *Activities:* Ocean swimming, deep-sea and river fishing, sailing, boat rental, tennis, and riding nearby. *How to get there:* The one street into Castletownsend ends at the harbor. Bow Hall is on the right-hand side.

ABBEYGLEN CASTLE HOTEL

> It is no hardship to stay at Clifden . . . I could go in-
> land among the purple mountains of Connemara, I
> could go south along the coast, following crescent after
> crescent of silver-sanded bays; bays where men from
> wrecked ships of the Spanish Armada once struggled
> ashore, bays where many a cask has been landed on
> a dark night.
>
> *Robert Gibbings*, 1945

Indeed it is no hardship to stay in Clifden, a pleasing town large enough to be lively but small enough to get to know. Nor is it a hardship to stay at the Abbeyglen Castle Hotel, where the hospitality is warm, the food is delicious, and spontaneous musical evenings happen.

This hotel on the Sky Road, on the edge of the town but an easy walk to the center, was an orphanage more than a hundred years ago, filled always to overflowing. That's hard to imagine today in this attractive mock castle. Windows look out over the pretty town, its graceful church spires dwarfed by silent mountains beyond.

Paul Hughes has developed a fine reputation for Abbeyglen's dining room. Locally caught fish—salmon, lobster, prawns, oysters, mussels, and scallops—are a specialty, and the kitchen will prepare all fish caught by guests. Besides the more usual appetizers, moussaka and a salad of prawn, walnut, celery, apple, and melon were on the menu. A choice of two soups is offered—lobster bisque and vegetable the day we were there. Roast beef with Yorkshire pudding is one memory, roast duckling with orange sauce another. A sweets trolley laden with home-made pastry, cake, a pudding, and fresh fruit is rolled up to your table, or you may request the cheese board. A comprehensive wine list includes clarets from famous chateaus, burgundies from the Rhone, hocks from the Rhine, and vintage port.

A swimming pool invites you to be lazy while you gaze at mountain and moor. Abbeyglen combines the joys of a country hotel, set in gardens and enjoying views, with the advantages of being in a town where you can saunter in and out of shops and pubs.

If we were to spend Christmas in Ireland, this is where we might stay. We would find cocktail parties, candlelit dinners, and musical evenings with dancing; a visit by Santa; golf and table-tennis tournaments; and services at both the Roman Catholic church and the Church of Ireland.

Price category: Moderate. *Proprietor:* Paul Hughes. *Telephone:* (095) 21201. *Closed:* January 10 through February 10. *Rooms:* 40 with bath, TV, and telephone; ground-floor rooms; 3-day reduction; Christmas and New Year's programs. *Meals:* Luncheon, snacks, tea, dinner for public; full license. *Facilities:* 2 lounges, cocktail bar, public bar, garden. *Activities:* Outdoor pool, tennis, pitch and putt, sauna, game room, movies and musical entertainment in season at the hotel; river and deep-sea fishing, ocean swimming, boat trips, and riding nearby. *Credit cards:* Amex, Diners, Master, Visa. *U.S. agent:* RS. *How to get there:* Clifden is on Route N59 on the west coast of Galway. Guests can be met at Shannon airport or the Galway railway station.[T]

Clifden, Galway

ARDAGH HOTEL

The whole of the western board of Ireland is washed by a sea as clear and blue as the finest sapphire. Nothing of the kind is to be seen on the shores of England.
Dr. James Johnson, 1844

The Ardagh Hotel faces the sea on the western coast of Connemara. Windows of the low modern building look out on pure nature. Sometimes otters swim in front of the hotel, and graceful herons stalk the rocky shore in search of small fish.

The hotel is owned by the Berings, a Dutch family. The restaurant is the pride of daughter Monique, who turns out food that is recommended by Michelin. All rooms are furnished in modern style in quiet colors. Picture windows in the dining room command views of spectacular sunsets, as do those of the spacious bar-lounge, a good place for socializing with house guests and locals before or after dinner. Big comfortable chairs furnish the lounge. Continental quilts cover the beds, but you can ask for sheets and blankets if you prefer them.

Nearby is the historic spot where John Alcock and Arthur Brown landed in a bog at the end of the first nonstop trans-atlantic flight in June 1919. A cairn has been erected there, and a monument on the roadside nearby marks the feat.

Price category: Moderate. *Proprietors:* The Berings family. *Telephone:* (095) 21384. *Closed:* November to Easter. *Rooms:* 17 with bath, TV, and telephone. *Meals:* Snacks (till 2 P.M.), tea (high season only), and dinner for public; full license. *Facilities:* Lounge, public bar, game room. *Activities:* Deep-sea fishing, ocean swimming, boat trips, boat rental, tennis, and riding nearby. *Credit cards:* Amex, Master, Visa. *How to get there:* The hotel is 1 1/2 miles south of Clifden toward Ballyconneely.

ROCK GLEN COUNTRY HOUSE HOTEL

There are views of the lakes and surrounding country
which the best parts of Killarney do not surpass, I think.
. . . The carriage road to Clifden is but ten years old
. . . streams and falls of water dash by everywhere . . .
and hard by are some of the finest bays in the world.
William Makepeace Thackeray, 1842

Just south of Clifden, on the carriage road that was new when Thackeray traveled these parts, Rock Glen captures the spirit of rural country-house hospitality. We find that the lodgings we most enjoy are those efficiently run by their owners; John and Evangeline Roche have worked hard to make this one a success. A welcoming fire burns in the lounge of this former hunting lodge. John's forte is the cooking. He was chef at prestigious Ashford Castle and is justly proud of his award-winning dining room, which provides the very best of good Irish food.

A long driveway leads to the hotel. The only sound you are likely to hear will be the mooing of cattle grazing beside a pond in the meadow that separates Rock Glen from the road. An intimate, well-stocked bar,

with views of mountain and sea, is a popular rendezvous where you will meet local people. Bedrooms in a modern wing are attractive and comfortable.

In August the lively Connemara Pony Show, combined with an exhibit of native arts and crafts, draws horse dealers from all over Ireland. Book well ahead for it.

Price category: Moderate. *Proprietors:* John and Evangeline Roche. *Telephone:* (095) 21035. *Closed:* November to mid-March. *Rooms:* 31 with bath and telephone. *Meals:* Snacks, dinner for public; full license. *Facilities:* Lounge, TV room, public bar, billiard room, garden. *Activities:* Floodlit tennis at the hotel; ocean, lake, and river swimming, deep-sea fishing, boat rental, boat trips, tennis, and riding nearby. *Credit cards:* Amex, Diners, Master, Visa. *U.S. agent:* RS. *How to get there:* The hotel is on Route R341 about 1 mile south of Clifden. Guests can be met at the bus in Clifden.

[T]

Clones, Monaghan

HILTON PARK

An old . . . family mansion is a fertile subject for study.
It abounds with illustrations of former times, and traces
of the tastes, and humors, and manners of successive
generations.

Washington Irving, 1822

Johnny Madden is the eighth generation of his family to live in this old
mansion, which does indeed "abound with the illustrations of former
times." This manor house, with antique furniture indicative of the splen-

dor of its past, is still elegant, if not kept today in the style to which Johnny's ancestors were accustomed, when hordes of servants did all the work. Rooms have ceilings of elaborate plaster work, and one room has wallpaper that went on in 1812. Bedrooms with enormous four-poster or tester beds, cheval mirrors, and chaise longues all offer views out over parkland.

Despite its grandeur, Hilton Park is a friendly and informal place. Johnny and Lucy Madden, who live here with their school-age children, are warm and welcoming. On part of the estate's large acreage, Johnny (and he is always Johnny, never John) raises cattle and sheep. A 9-hole golf course on the place has become a golf club for residents of the area.

Lucy does most of the cooking herself, using meat, fresh vegetables, and dairy products from the farm. Breads and pastries are home--baked. Don't miss her homemade cream cheese, one of several cheeses she makes that have won prizes at agricultural fairs. Be sure to let her know in advance if you'll want dinner.

Groups of four to six people who reserve ahead get a large reduction from the prices given in our index for an overnight stay. In the winter Johnny offers house parties for rough shooting over woodlands and three lakes. All meals are included, and the lifestyle is that of bygone days. Write for details.

Hilton Park is a place worth going out of your way for. Staying here is so much like staying with friends that you'll probably want to send a thank-you note when you get home.

Price category: Moderate to expensive. *Proprietors:* Lucy and Johnny Madden. *Telephone:* (047) 56007. *Closed:* October to April. *Rooms:* 6, 2 with bath. *Meals:* Dinner for guests. *Facilities:* Sitting room, garden. *Activities:* Golf, lake swimming, boating, and fishing for pike and trout at the house; riding and boat rental nearby. *Credit card:* Amex. *U.S. agent:* Robert Reid Associates. *How to get there:* From the town of Monaghan, take Route N54 southwest to Clones (pronounced Clo ness').

Clonmel, Tipperary

KNOCKLOFTY HOUSE

> What a lovely thing the country is! . . . the heart of
> Tipperary, the Golden Vein. The country that Crom-
> well gazed on and acclaimed: "A land well worth
> winning."
>
> *Anonymous*

This splendid estate was home until 1982 to the Earls of Donoughmore,
to whom Cromwell granted most of the lands of County Tipperary in
1640. Today it is one of Ireland's most beautiful hotels. Set in 105 acres
of rolling parkland, the classical mansion was begun in 1720 and added
to over the centuries.

The old-world beauty of the exterior is matched within. High ceilings are embellished with delicate plasterwork. Room after room is furnished with well-chosen antiques, Oriental rugs, and fine fabrics.
Candlelight complements original oak paneling in the dining room. Our
favorite room is the large library, where there's a log fire and a grand

piano. It is two stories high with a balcony all around, with oak ladders that roll to reach books on four walls of floor-to-ceiling shelves.

You must reserve to have luncheon or dinner, but you can drop in for afternoon tea. We like to have it on the terrace, an idyllic setting in good weather, where the River Suir tumbles along right in front. Across, cattle graze in lush fields backed by hazy mountains.

Fishing gear is available if you want to try for salmon or trout. The Tipperary hunt meets at Knocklofty House several times a season, a colorful sight even if you don't hunt. Some of the buildings on the estate have become time-share units, which accounts for the unusual sporting facilities available to this small elegant hotel of friendly informality.

Price category: Expensive to very expensive. *Proprietors:* Joyce and Paddy O'Keefe. *Telephone:* (052) 38222. *Rooms:* 11 with bath; suitable for wheelchair guests. *Meals:* Luncheon (by reservation), tea, dinner (by reservation) to public; full license. *Facilities:* Drawing room, library, cocktail bar, snooker room, garden. *Activities:* Indoor pool, tennis, exercise room, squash, solarium, jacuzzi, fishing (with fly-fishing courses), riding, and golf driving range at the house; rough shooting with local gun club, riding, and hunting nearby. *Credit cards:* Amex, Master, Visa. *How to get there:* Knocklofty is 4 miles southwest of Clonmel on route R665.   [T]

MARKREE CASTLE

> I longed for something of Sligo . . . it was our mother, who kept alive that love. She would spend hours telling stories of her own Sligo girlhood, and it was always assumed between her and us that Sligo was more beautiful than other places.
>
> *William Butler Yeats,* 1915

Yeats was a regular visitor to Markree Castle, the home of the Cooper family for over 300 years. In the center of a 1000-acre estate, the castle is considered one of Ireland's major architectural masterpieces.

Charles and Mary Cooper gained experience in several countries before returning to Sligo to open Knockmuldowney Restaurant, now recommended in Michelin and all leading food guides. It's success enabled them to buy Markree Castle from Charles's brother, turn it into a hotel, and move the restaurant to it.

The Coopers restored the castle but added good modern heating and bathrooms. Reception room ceilings are richly decorated with plasterwork, and a magnificent oak staircase leads to bedrooms, some of them very large, furnished with antiques.

Entrées on the menu might range from poached salmon to baked stuffed pork chops or Hungarian beef goulash. Start, perhaps, with mushroom and walnut pâté, continue with carrot and orange soup, and choose rhubarb brulee or chocolate praline cream for dessert, followed by an all-Irish cheese board. The wine list numbers almost 200 varieties.

A friend who has traveled extensively in Ireland wrote of Knockmuldowney House, "The food was probably the best I have had in Ireland, the Coopers extremely helpful and pleasant. Absolutely and without exception first rate." The same standard that earned Knockmuldowney House such a reputation is continued in the new, historic surroundings.

Price category: Expensive. *Proprietors:* Charles and Mary Cooper. *Telephone:* (071) 67800. *Closed:* Two weeks in February. *Rooms:* 15 with bath and telephone; TV available. *Meals:* Dinner for public; full license. *Facilities:* Reception lounge, sitting room, library, garden. *Activities:* Ocean swimming, tennis, and riding nearby. *U.S. agent:* Robert Reid. *How to get there:* Signposted at junction of N4 and N17, 7 miles south of Sligo town.   [T]

Cong, Mayo

ASHFORD CASTLE HOTEL

> If any one, like Mary McMahon of County Clare, who
> had twenty-five husbands, one at a time, should need
> a permanent honeymoon address they could not do
> better than Ashford Castle.
>
> *Robert Gibbings*, 1945

'The architecture is daft . . . false crenellations, blind machicolations, useless bartizans everywhere," continues Gibbings. Ashford Castle looks like every child's image of what a castle should be. Its castellated facade incorporates the remains of a thirteenth-century Norman castle, an eighteenth-century French chateau, and a Victorian mock castle built by Sir Benjamin Guinness of the brewery fortune. Entrance to the estate is over a drawbridge and portcullised gateway under a great turreted tower.

Ashford Castle is among Europe's most deluxe. Its lavish interior wholly matches the impressive exterior. Formal gardens are set in an extensive acreage of lawns and woodlands bordering Lough Corrib, world-renowned for its trout and salmon fishing. The movie *The Quiet Man* was filmed on the grounds. A nine-hole golf course is reserved for guests at the castle.

King Edward VII slept here in 1905, and legend has it that a wing with a billiard room was built just for his visit because he so enjoyed the game. The king and his shooting party killed ninety brace of woodcock in one day. Those who would like to follow his example can try, as Ashford offers rough shooting over thousands of acres for pheasant, snipe, duck, and woodcock. It has associations with Oscar Wilde and his father, Sir William, who were visitors and lived nearby. A more recent visitor was President Ronald Reagan, in 1984.

Cong is a tiny village surrounding the ruins of Cong Abbey, where Rory O'Connor — the last high king of Ireland before the Norman invasion — died in 1198. A stay at Ashford Castle is a pleasing date with history for those who like a hotel atmosphere with all modern luxuries.

Price category: Very expensive. *Manager:* Rory Murphy. *Telephone:* (092) 46003. *Rooms:* 77 with bath, telephone, and TV; 6 suites; elevator. *Meals:* Luncheon, snacks, tea, dinner for public; full license. *Children:* Baby-sitting and -listening. *Facilities:* 2 lounges, TV lounge, sun parlor, cocktail bar, gift shop, hair salon, garden. *Activities:* Salmon and trout fishing, clay-pigeon shooting school, free golf and tennis, game room, and musical entertainment at the hotel. *Credit cards:* Amex, Diners, Master, Visa. *U.S. agent:* Ashford Castle, MC. *How to get there:* The hotel is on Route R345 in Cong.   [T]

ARBUTUS LODGE HOTEL

> The spreading Lee that, like an island fayre,
> Encloseth Cork with his divided floode.
> *Edmund Spenser,* 1598

The center of Cork is actually an island, the old city that Edmund Spenser knew. Arbutus Lodge, a much modernized Georgian house, sits on a hillside overlooking the old city. While the view over Cork would be one good reason to eat in its window-walled bar or in the bay window of the dining room, if you could capture that choice location, the big attraction here is the food. If there were a prize given for the best restaurant in all of Ireland, Arbutus Lodge would be high among the finalists and might win the blue ribbon. It is one of two in Ireland to receive Michelin stars, and the wine list won an award as the best in Britain and Ireland. A large tank in the bar holds live lobsters and oysters, with a scale to weigh the lobster chosen. Service is at once professional and friendly.

Memories of Georgian days survive in the decorating, strongest in the large entrance foyer that is painted cocoa brown on walls and ceiling, with lavishly curlicued plaster work painted white in sharp contrast. The public rooms contain many antique pieces. Bedrooms with quality modern furniture are fitted ingeniously into every nook and cranny and come in widely varied sizes and shapes. Check the weekend rate—any two nights for two people, with dinner included one night.

Exceptional tiered gardens lead down to a car park, a good place to leave your car during your visit to Cork. You might enjoy a walk down into town, but we think you'll want to use the frequent bus service to come back up those hills. The hotel has a direct line to the taxi rank.

Price category: Expensive to very expensive. *Proprietors:* The Ryan family. *Telephone:* (021) 501237. *Rooms:* 20 with bath and telephone; weekend breaks. *Meals:* Luncheon, snacks, tea, dinner for public; full license. *Children:* Baby-sitting. *Facilities:* TV room, cocktail bar, garden. *Credit cards:* Amex, Diners, Master, Visa. *Mailing address:* Arbutus Lodge, Montenotte, Cork, County Cork. *How to get there:* Arbutus Lodge is a short walk uphill from the railway station. If carrying luggage, you'd probably want a taxi. [T]

GABRIEL HOUSE

> On this I ponder, where'er I wander,
> And thus grow fonder, Sweet Cork, of thee;
> With thy bells of Shandon, that sound so grand on
> The pleasant waters of the River Lee.
>
> *Francis Mahoney (Father Prout),* 1851

Not long ago Gabriel House was a dwelling for the Irish Christian Brothers. Now it is an attractive guest house that is less expensive than city hotels. Some of its freshly decorated bedrooms have fine views over Cork city. A night porter is in attendance, and light refreshments are available around the clock. There's a pleasant garden where you can sit and watch city lights come on after a day's sight-seeing and shopping.

You'd do well to leave your car in the parking lot here while you explore Cork. The guest house is within walking distance of the city center, and buses give frequent service. As Gabriel House is just a walk away from the railway station, it is a fine choice for those traveling by train.

Price category: Inexpensive. *Proprietor:* Monica King. *Telephone:* (021) 500333. *Rooms:* 20 with bath, TV, and telephone; ground-floor rooms. *Meals: Snacks and dinner for guests. Children:* Baby-sitting; reduction. *Facilities:* Lounge, garden. *Mailing address:* Summerhill, St. Luke's, Cork, County Cork. *How to get there:* From the railway station turn left toward the city. Cross the road to a footbridge and walkway. Take the walkway to Summerhill Street, and turn right. Or take the number-8 bus from the city center.

LOTAMORE HOUSE

> Cork is the loveliest city in the world. Anybody who doesn't agree with me either was not born there or is prejudiced.
>
> *Robert Gibbings,* 1945

This Georgian manor guest house is on the outskirts of Cork, but only a four-minute drive from the center. A graceful stairway and rich

plasterwork on high ceilings speak of another age, but the furnishings, in quiet colors and good taste, are new, as is the central heat. The soft coral color of the lounge complements the white-and-coral marble fireplace, where a log fire burns. From large windows you can see Blackrock Castle and the harbor in the distance. Guests can order snacks or afternoon tea served here at any time of day or evening. Large bedrooms are fitted with comfortable unit furniture and have excellent modern bathrooms, each with a tub and a shower.

The only meal served at Lotamore House, which has no liquor license, is breakfast, but guests can take a path to a good restaurant called Hunter's Lodge, next door, without walking out onto the highway.

Price category: Inexpensive. *Proprietors:* Ken and Mairead Harty. *Telephone:* (021) 822344. *Rooms:* 20 with bath, telephone, and TV; suitable for wheel-chair guests. *Children:* Baby-sitting. *Facilities:* Lounge and garden. *Credit cards:* Amex, Master, Visa. *Mailing address:* Tivoli, Cork. *How to get there:* Lotamore House is on the main Cork-Dublin–Waterford double-lane highway, just beyond the Silver Springs Hotel, traveling east.　　　　　　　　　　　　　　[T]

Courtmacsherry, Cork

COURTMACSHERRY HOTEL

Will not an inn his cares beguile
Where on each face he sees a smile.
William Combe, 1781

Watching the sun go down over Courtmacsherry Bay would be reason enough for a stay at this gracious hotel. The food that owner-chef Terry Adams prepares might be an even better one. Once here, you will like walking along the peaceful woodland paths that lead from the hotel along the bay to secluded swimming spots, or watching the great variety of sea and wading birds; but most of all you will enjoy the friendly hospitality.

The house was built in 1820 as a summer residence by Lady Charlotte Boyle, a descendant of the earl of Cork who built Lismore Castle. A cork tree reported to be more than 150 years old stands among the rhododendron and palm trees on its 10 acres. Terry Adams came from England in 1974 to buy Courtmacsherry. His father, who helps out, has a warm personality that makes guests feel like old friends. He will give advice on what to do and where to go and will help map routes to get there. His watercolors, mainly of local scenes, adorn the walls of the high-ceilinged lounge where big, comfortable velvet chairs and a sofa rest on an Aubusson-type rug. Many handsome coffee-table books about Ireland mix with English *Country Life* magazines. There are just a few antique pieces here and there, but somehow the effect is more Old World than this assortment should warrant.

For a small hotel, there is an unusually extensive, but reasonably priced, wine list. Cooking has earned compliments in food guides. Displayed in the bar, a good stop for a snack lunch, is a sonar depth recording of the sunken *Lusitania*, which was torpedoed just 10 miles off Courtmacsherry in April 1915 with great loss of life. Rescue boats from the Courtmacsherry coast guard station brought in survivors. In July 1979, boats went out again from this station to rescue survivors from the ill-fated Cowes-Fastnet sailing race.

Price category: Inexpensive. *Proprietor:* Terry Adams. *Telephone:* (023) 46198. *Closed:* October to Easter. *Rooms:* 15, 9 with bath; 3-day reduction. *Meals:* Snacks, tea, dinner for public; full license. *Children:* Baby-sitting; pony; reduction. *Facilities:* Lounge, TV room, cocktail bar, smoking room, garden. *Activities:* Tennis and riding at the hotel; ocean swimming, and deep-sea fishing nearby. *U.S. agent:* RS. *How to get there:* Take Route R602 south from Bandon. Guests can be met at the Cork airport or railway station.

Crossmolina, Mayo

ENNISCOE HOUSE

> Here might be found old . . . houses in the style of
> antique English manorial chateaus . . . displaying, in
> the dwelling rooms, a comfort and cosiness combined
> with magnificence, not always so effectually attained
> in modern times.
>
> *Thomas De Quincey,* 1802

De Quincey writes that when he visited his school friend Lord Westport in 1801, they traveled from Dublin to Westport House, Mayo, "making many leisurely deviations from the direct route." Enniscoe House could have been one of the great houses at which they spent a night along the way. At that time, well-off travelers stayed with relatives or friends, or even friends of friends. Hospitality was unbounded; everyone welcomed guests, grateful for a break in their isolation and happy to exchange news.

To enter Enniscoe House is to step directly into history. In 1798, a French force landed nearby at Killala Bay to help the Irish in one of their more famous attempts to throw off the English. On a march south, the French stopped here at Enniscoe House to eat and rest. According to Mrs. Kellett, family history records that the French officers drank all the fine wine stored in her ancestors' cellar. The story of the French landing and march are told in the novel *Year of the French.*

Sheep and beef cattle are raised on this 300-acre estate. The house is surrounded by wooded parkland, part of which is called French Avenue. It has its own jetty on bordering Lough Conn and two small lake islands, one with a ruined fifteenth-century castle.

The house is still elegant, with very high ceilings embellished with rococo plasterwork. It has been designated a Heritage House of Ireland. A formal drawing room, where French furniture is covered with pale blue brocade, still has its 1840 wallpaper, upon which hang ancestor portraits. Another living room, although large, is cozy, with comfortable furniture grouped before a friendly fire. A curved staircase rises under an architecturally unique glass dome.

Some of the enormous main bedrooms, with private bathrooms that are larger than many a bedroom in which we've stayed, have four-poster beds with draw-curtains and offer views over lough and fields. Boats are available for rent, and an experienced ghillie can take you fishing.

Price category: Moderate. *Proprietor:* Mrs. Susan Kellett. *Telephone:* (096) 31112. *Closed:* October through March. *Rooms:* 7, 5 with bath; self-catering cottage. *Meals:* Dinner for public by reservation; wine license. *Children:* Baby-sitting. *Facilities:* Drawing room, living room, sitting room, garden. *Activities:* Trout and pike fishing, boat rental, and woodcock shoots at the estate; ocean swimming, salmon fishing, deep-sea fishing, tennis, and riding nearby. *Credit cards:* Amex, Master, Visa. *U.S. agent:* Robert Reid Associates. *How to get there:* The house is on Route R315, 2 miles south of Crossmolina.   [T]

LAHARDAN HOUSE

> I feel more strongly with every recurring year that our
> country has no tradition which does it so much honour
> . . .as that of its hospitality. It is a tradition that is
> unique as far as my experience goes (and I have visited
> not a few places abroad) among the modern nations.
> *James Joyce,* 1928

You will be met with fine hospitality at Lahardan House by Dilly
Griffey, former secretary of the Irish Farm Holidays Association. This
group of owners of some of the nicest Irish farm homes that take guests
have helped each other learn how best to please their visitors without
disrupting farm and family work. Because of their efforts, Irish farm
homes today enjoy a reputation for offering some of the best
bed-and-breakfast lodgings in Europe. And in Ireland, unlike America, most bed-and-breakfast accommodations, including this one, offer dinner or supper, called high tea (but let each hostess know about
noon if you'll want it).

This old-fashioned farmhouse with a modern extension is in a peaceful valley not far north of Shannon Airport. Known for its food, it
would be a good place to stay for a few days while you tour the beautiful coast of Clare, see the Cliffs of Moher, and explore the weird Burren landscape. You can go east to Lough Derg and take a one-day cruise
on the River Shannon. Lahardan House is central to three castles that
regularly offer medieval banquets — Bunratty, Knappogue, and Dun-
guaire.

Price category: Very inexpensive. *Proprietors:* Dilly and Tom
Griffey. *Telephone:* (065) 27128. *Rooms:* 9 with bath; ground-floor
rooms. *Meals:* Dinner for guests; wine license. *Children:* Baby-sitting;
playground. *Facilities:* Sitting room, TV room, garden. *Activities:* Lake
swimming, rowboat rental, coarse and game fishing, riding, and hunting nearby. *How to get there:* The farm is about a mile and a half from
Crusheen Village, where it is signposted on Route N18.

CLEEVAUN

> . . . a splendour that was almost a grief in the mind.
> *John Millington Synge,* 1907

When playwright Synge wrote the words above, he was describing the beauty of the spectacular Dingle peninsula. While you explore its wild coast and magnificent scenery, Cleevaun would be a good choice for bed-and-breakfast lodging.

A rock garden bright with flowers beside a manicured lawn makes an inviting approach. Charlotte Cluskey will give you a warm welcome to her modern home. A comfortable lounge with an electric fire has books about the area hospitably laid out for guests. From the breakfast room, you'll enjoy a view across fields to Dingle Bay, a fine start for the day. Ask for a bedroom with this same view. Bathrooms have showers, and some have bidets. A breakfast menu offers many choices. No dinner is served, but Dingle has two of Ireland's top restaurants, as well as others that provide good fare.

Nearby is the Gallarus oratory, the most perfectly preserved early Christian church in Ireland, made of unmortared stone still completely watertight after more than a thousand years.

Price category: Very inexpensive. *Proprietor:* Charlotte Cluskey. *Telephone:* (066) 51108. *Closed:* November to Easter. *Rooms:* 5 with bath; ground-floor rooms. *Children:* Not suitable for those under 11. *Facilities:* Living room, garden. *Activities:* Ocean swimming, deep-sea fishing, boat trips, boat rental, and riding nearby. *How to get there:* Cleevaun is about half a mile west of Dingle on Route R559.

DOYLE'S TOWNHOUSE

> Quality is never an accident, it is always the result of intelligent effort.
>
> *John Ruskin,* 1853

The quality of Doyle's Restaurant made it known as one of the best in Ireland. Now the efforts of Stella and John Doyle are responsible for the fine quality of the guest house they have opened in the house adjoining their restaurant.

Although it is right in the little town, a country-house atmosphere prevails. You enter into a living room warmed by the red of an Oriental rug. The Doyles chased auctions and sales around Ireland and found a fine craftsman to restore the old pieces they bought. All rooms are furnished with antiques and lovely fabrics. The house was built in 1830, but doors salvaged from an 18th-century house now lead into the bedrooms, most of which have a sofa that will make a bed for a third person. Rooms on the top floor have large skylights and views over fields. Bathrooms have both shower and tub, and some offer bidets too.

The Townhouse door will be locked from mid-November to mid-March to those who come knocking, but if you want to visit Dingle at that time, you can telephone. If John and Stella are to be there, they'll be happy to have you, except at Christmas time.

In its sixteenth-century heyday, Dingle was a walled town and a center of trade with Spain. The remains of a ship of the Spanish Armada—the Santa Maria de la Rosa—lies under the ocean nearby. Today Dingle is a fishing port where colorful lobster traps are piled on docks and fishing boats unload their catch each evening. From Doyle's Townhouse, it's easy to walk to the waterfront and all about the little town, which has many good shops.

Price category: Moderate. *Proprietors:* John and Stella Doyle. *Telephone:* (066) 51174. *Closed:* Mid-November to mid-March, except by reservation. *Rooms:* 8 with bath, telephone, and TV; ground-floor rooms. *Meals:* Lunch and dinner to public except Sunday. *Facilities:* Living room and garden. *Activities:* Ocean swimming, deep-sea fishing, boat trips, boat rental, and riding nearby. *Credit cards:* Master, Visa. *U.S. agent:* Robert Reid. *How to get there:* Drive through the few streets of Dingle and you'll spot Doyle's. [T]

SKELLIG HOTEL

> . . . the bars of silvery light breaking through on the
> further inlets of the bay, had the singularly brilliant
> liveliness one meets everywhere in Kerry.
>
> *John Millington Synge,* 1907

The Dingle peninsula must be one of the most beautiful places in the
world—cobalt-blue sea, rocky headlands, stark mountains, roads lined
with crimson fuchsia hedges.

The Skellig Hotel is a fairly large place of many services from which
to explore the peninsula. Its modern facade is undistinguished, but once
inside the door you'll find a handsome, inviting interior. A window-walled lounge, with a big stone fireplace where a turf fire burns,
is decorated in beautiful colors. Attractive modern bedrooms with wood
ceilings have good reading lights. The Coastguard Restaurant, em-
phasizing fresh seafood, has a view that stretches across Dingle Bay
to the mountains of the Ring of Kerry. Rooms are enhanced by hand-
crafted lamps, wall hangings, and original paintings. Sometimes there
is traditional entertainment by local musicians in the convivial bar.

The many activities available make this a good place for children
and young people. They can take sailing and windsurfing lessons right
from the hotel. Tennis courts are floodlit, and the large indoor pool
has a wall of windows.

A five-minute walk takes you into Dingle, the westernmost town
in Europe. Ryans Daughter was filmed in the surrounding area.

Price category: Moderate. *Manager:* Sean Cluskey. *Telephone:* (066)
51144. *Closed:* November through February. *Rooms:* 70 with bath, telephone, and TV; suitable for wheel-chair guests; breaks. *Meals:* Luncheon, snacks, tea, dinner to public; full license. *Children:* Baby-sitting
and -listening; playground. *Facilities:* Lounge, cocktail bar, games
room, terrace. *Activities:* Indoor pool, exercise room, tennis, pitch and
putt, sauna, jumbo chess, sailing and windsurfing schools at hotel;
shore fishing, deep-sea fishing, ocean swimming, boat rental, boat trips,
and riding nearby. *Credit cards:* Amex, Diners, Master, Visa. *U.S.
agent:* Quality. *How to get there:* Hotel is signposted on Route T68 as
you enter Dingle. [T]

Donegal

ERNAN PARK

> To hear the whisper of small waves
> against the rocks, that endless sea-
> sound, like keening over graves.
>
> *St. Columcille,* 6th century
> (translated from the Gaelic)

The fragrance of the sea floats into every room at this small hotel on St. Ernan's Island, whose 8 1/2 acres are joined to the mainland by a short causeway. After a climb up a rather long outside stairway bordered with flowers, guests are warmed by a fire in the reception hall.

Marble mantels, bay windows, and a good supply of books and antiques are features of the well-furnished rooms in this 1826 house. Another fire glows in a dining room that entices residents of Donegal. Every window of the house affords a view of the sea, in changing shades of blue and green as it flows back and forth with the tide. These waters are the haunt of the curlews, the oyster catchers, and the black-headed gulls. Watch them swoop and dive, and listen to their cries.

Price category: Moderate. *Proprietor:* Brian O'Dowd. *Telephone:* (073) 21065. *Closed:* November to Easter. *Rooms:* 11 with bath, telephone, and TV. *Children:* Not recommended under 6. *Meals:* Dinner to the public; full license. *Facilities:* Lounge, cocktail lounge with TV, garden. *Activities:* Ocean swimming at the house. *U.S. agent:* RS. *How to get there:* Ernan Park is signposted on Route N15, 1 mile south of Donegal. [T]

HYLAND CENTRAL HOTEL

Oh my small town of Ireland, the raindrops caress you,
The sun sparkles bright on your field and your Square
As here on your bridge I salute you and bless you,
Your murmuring waters and turf-scented air.

John Betjeman

Right in the center of the small market town of Donegal, between the square and the murmuring waters of the River Eske where it flows into Donegal Bay, is one of Ireland's best-run, modern, town hotels, the Hyland Central. The atmosphere is that of a professional hotel, but friendly. There is no sitting room other than a large comfortable bar-lounge where you can order delicious pub food. Agreeable bedrooms have unit furniture, the ones in the back with good views of the river and bay. Readers might find it an interesting change from country-house hotels and small guest houses.

Shopping is right outside the door and all around the square, which is actually a diamond. One place not to miss is Magee of Donegal, a company that has been making handwoven tweed since 1866. At their retail store, they carry a good selection of ready-to-wear tweed clothes for men and women, but you'll see bolts of tweed in such irresistible colors that you'll want to buy it by the yard to have clothes made up when you get home. (Come prepared with the yardage amounts needed. We even sent some home to use for upholstering.) The tweed is still woven in cottages in the countryside, then finished at a factory in town that you can tour.

A short walk away is the ruin of a Jacobean castle once home to the O'Donnells who ruled this region.

Price category: Moderate. *Proprietor:* Liam Hyland. *Telephone:* (073) 21027. *Closed:* 3 days at Christmas. *Rooms:* 59 with bath, telephone, and TV; elevator; weekend breaks off season. *Meals:* Luncheon, snacks, tea, and dinner to the public; full license. *Children:* Baby-sitting and -listening. *Facilities:* Cocktail lounge, garden. *Activities:* Ocean swimming, tennis, and boat trips nearby. *Credit cards:* Amex, Master, Visa. *U.S. agent:* Best Western. *How to get there:* The hotel is on Route N15. [T]

Drinagh, Wexford

KILLIANE CASTLE HOUSE

> A nodding Norman keep
> Telling with scattered walls and scars
> A rugged tale of great old war
> And warriors long asleep.   *Anonymous*

This imposing farmhouse, a manor built in the early seventeenth century, is now the home of the Mernaghs, who operate a large dairy farm on 230 acres. The ruin of an adjoining thirteenth-century castle fortress bears testimony to the building genius of the Normans. A great demesne here once belonged to descendants of the earl of Somerset, brother of Jane Seymour and Lord Protector for his nephew, the boy king Edward VI.

Velvet-covered Victorian sofas, marble-topped tables, polished brass fireside accessories, and many books furnish the gracious living rooms. Bedrooms are plain and small, bathrooms are tiled, and everything is very well maintained. Warm hospitality and good home-cooking are assured. In July and August, rooms are usually taken by the week. Ireland's former Prime Minister Garrett Fitzgerald was a guest here.

In the courtyard of the old castle are are four modern units, each with living room, kitchenette, bedroom, and bath. Those who rent them may use the tennis court and putting green on the farm.

Killiane Castle is in the sunniest and driest part of Ireland. Long sandy beaches and a championship golf course are nearby. In the town of Wexford, members of the Old Wexford Society conduct walking tours of the historic winding streets. Evening entertainment at hotels includes a *Seisiun*, a program of traditional Irish entertainment, and a dinner theater.

Price category: Very inexpensive. *Proprietors:* Kathleen and Jack Mernagh. *Telephone:* (053) 58885. *Closed:* November 8 through March. *Rooms:* 8, 2 with bath; ground-floor rooms; self-catering apartments. *Meals:* Dinner for guests; wine license. *Children:* Baby-sitting; children's meals; pony; playground. *Facilities:* Lounge, TV room, garden. *Activities:* Tennis and putting green at the house; ocean swimming, and riding nearby. *How to get there:* The house is signposted about 3 miles south of Wexford on Route N25. Turn left and go about half a mile.

HARBOUR VILLA

> Hospitality is no word for the overflowing welcome
> which was invariably extended to a stranger in Ireland.
> *M. E. Haworth,* 1882

Sheila and Tommy Dwyer offer a true Irish welcome at Harbour Villa, their old-style country home on the River Boyne, just a mile from the ancient town of Drogheda.

Their garden is their pride. An unusual feature is a garden house containing a sun lounge where guests can bask out of the wind while admiring the flowers. There is also a grass court for some lazy tennis, although good players would probably prefer to play on the hard courts available at a nearby tennis club.

Inside the vine-covered Harbour Villa, plain furnishings are mixed with some good antiques, including a display of polished silver in the dining room. The bedrooms are small and plainly furnished. Those who value old-time homeyness and hospitality more than hotel luxury will find it a pleasant stop.

Five miles away are the remains of Monasterboice, a fifth-century abbey, which has one of the most nearly perfect high crosses in Ireland. This early-tenth-century cross is more than 17 feet tall, and almost every inch of its surface is ornamented with sculptured panels depicting scenes from the Gospels. The remains of a round tower, once the tallest in Ireland, can be explored at the abbey.

Price category: Very inexpensive. *Proprietors:* Sheila and Tommy Dwyer. *Telephone:* (041) 37441. *Rooms:* 4 with shared baths. *Meals:* Dinner for guests; no license. *Children:* Baby-sitting; swing. *Facilities:* Sitting room, TV room, garden. *Activities:* Ocean swimming, indoor pool, tennis, squash, sea and river fishing, and riding nearby. *Mailing address:* Harbour Villa, Mornington Road, Drogheda, County Louth. *How to get there:* The house is on Route R150 east of Drogheda.

AISLING

> In Dublin . . . the traveller falls into a mood of uncritical enthusiasm. Fresh from the world beyond . . . he feels that he has entered a little haven of peace and joy.
> *Honor Tracy,* 1953

At Aisling, the Mooney family provides a little haven on the north side of Dublin, the part of the city nearest to the airport. Mary Mooney is a warm and gracious hostess. Her century-old home, formerly a duplex, is nicely furnished, with some antique pieces in the living and dining rooms. Bedrooms have unit furniture to make the most of the available space, and some without private baths have corner showers. She'll suggest nearby places for dinner.

In the evening, Mr. Mooney frequently joins guests in the living room or in the garden in good weather. Tea and cookies are served, a nice custom. Aisling, half a block from the harbor, is a superior city private-home lodging.

Price category: Very inexpensive. *Proprietor:* Mrs. Mary Mooney. *Telephone:* (01) 339097. *Rooms:* 9, 5 with bath and telephone. *Children:* Baby-sitting. *Facilities:* Living room, garden, parking. *Mailing Address:* 20 St. Lawrence Rd, Clontarf, Dublin 3, Ireland. *How to get there:* From the airport, drive towards Dublin. After you see a large red brick church on your left, at next traffic lights turn left onto Collins Ave. Drive to the end and turn right onto Howth Rd. Take the second turn left and you will be on St Lawrence Rd. House is on the right. From Dublin center, take bus 30 or 44A.

ANGLESEA

In Dublin . . . pleasant ways of speech and manner
have not yet been forgotten; the gentleness, the warmth,
the quick sympathy with the stranger, turn every chance
contact into a source of pleasure.

Honor Tracy, 1953

Pleasant ways of speech and manner are still commonly found in
Dublin, nowhere more than at Anglesea. The house is Edwardian, built
in 1903. A flower-bordered walk leads to its stained-glass entrance door.
You'll be greeted upon arrival with tea and scones in the parlor, brought
to you by gentle Helen Kirrane.

The house is well furnished. The parlor has some Victorian pieces,
the dining room is in Chippendale style, stairs are carpeted, and bedrooms have pretty flowered draperies. Some of them overlook a cricket
ground. Mrs. Kirrane turns on electric blankets early in the evening so
the beds will be warm. She has won a "Best Breakfast" award from
the Irish Tourist Board and will cook you one as early as is necessary
for you to catch planes, trains, or boats, but she serves no dinner or
spirits.

This attractive guest house is in Ballsbridge, close to central Dublin.
The Berkeley Court and Jury's hotels are an easy walk away. If you
ever plan to attend Dublin's famous horse show, reserve here well ahead
and walk to the Royal Dublin Show Grounds nearby.

Price category: Moderate. *Proprietor:* Mrs. Helen Kirrane. *Tele-
phone:* (01) 683877. *Rooms:* 7 with bath, telephone, and TV. *Children:*
Child-sitting; not suitable for those under 8. *Facilities:* Living room,
garden. *Mailing address:* 63 Anglesea Road, Dublin 4. *How to get there:*
From the American Embassy, continue along Merrion Road. Anglesea
Road is the second right. The house is on the right.

ARIEL HOUSE

If you would have guests merry with cheer
Be so yourself or at least so appear.
Benjamin Franklin

You won't find a more cheerful and helpful man in Dublin than Michael O'Brien, your host at Ariel House, which is renowned for hospitality in a country where gracious hospitality is the rule. For five years Michael lived in San Francisco, where he worked at the outstanding Fairmont and Saint Francis hotels.

Ariel House radiates warmth and enthusiasm. Michael delights in seeing his guests enjoy themselves. He not only will help you plan for Dublin but also will chat with you about where you might go and what you might see in all Ireland, recommending good lodgings along the way. He was president of the Irish Guesthouse Association, and his own is meticulously maintained. You won't feel more at home in any lodging; yet the atmosphere is that of a small professional hotel. Although it seems as if he never leaves the place, Michael and his family have a separate home.

The main building is a mansion built for a marquis in 1850. An addition of very comfortable modern bedrooms extends to the rear. A parking area is behind this, with a ramp for wheelchairs.

The original Victorian drawing room is furnished with antiques and lit by a Waterford chandelier. When we are in Dublin, it is impossible for us to see all the relatives and friends we'd like to unless we gather them together in one place. Michael arranged for us to have a party in this drawing room. We had the feeling of being in a private home, with a location that was easy to reach. A no-smoking dining room with Victorian antique furniture, extended by a conservatory, overlooks the garden. Guests can order light supper items in the wine bar.

In the stylish Ballsbridge section, within a block of the well-known Jury's Hotel, Ariel House is but steps away from the Dart train, one stop out from the city center. Once travelers find it, they'll be unlikely to stay anywhere else in Dublin.

Price category: Moderate. *Proprietor:* Michael O'Brien. *Telephone:* (01) 685512. *Closed:* Mid-December through December 31. *Rooms:* 30 with bath, telephone, and TV; 2-day minimum advance reservation; suitable for wheelchair guests. *Children:* Not suitable. *Facilities:* Drawing room, wine bar, parking. *Smoking:* Not permitted in dining room. *Activities:* Tennis, squash, sauna, and ocean swimming nearby. *Mailing address:* 52 Lansdowne Road, Dublin 4. *How to get there:* Lansdowne Road begins at Jury's Hotel. Ariel House is in the middle of the second block from there. Take the Dart train or bus 5, 6, 7, or 8 from the city center. [T]

BUSWELL'S HOTEL

> This appears to be a very magnificent city. The streets
> we came through . . . contain a number of public
> buildings of the finest architecture I have seen
> anywhere in Britain.
>> *John Lockhart,* 1825

In the midst of the same fine public buildings that impressed John Lockhart, Buswell's is one of the most conveniently located hotels in Dublin. It is surrounded by a concentrated and fashionable shopping district. We like to make short sorties to the stores, buy a few things at a time, drop them back in our room, and be able to enjoy Dublin's architectural and historic attractions without carrying packages.

Guests receive a friendly welcome and personal attention at Buswell's, the oldest family-owned and -operated hotel in the city. Floral fabrics brighten the bedrooms, some of them smallish but with thoughtful extras like tea- and coffee-making facilities and hair dryers. The airy Georgian bar-lounge is a popular meeting place, particularly for members of Dail Eireann (Ireland's House of Parliament), which is just across the street. Trinity University, founded by Queen Elizabeth I, is a block away; the National Library, Museum, and Art Gallery are to the right. St. Stephen's Green, one of Europe's oldest city parks, is just around the corner. If you favor a city-center hotel at less than top rates, this is your best choice.

Price category: Expensive. *Proprietor:* Noel Duff. *Telephone:* (01) 764013. *Rooms:* 70, with bath, telephone, TV, and tea-making; elevator; winter weekend breaks. *Meals:* Luncheon, snacks, tea, dinner to the public; full license. *Facilities:* Cocktail lounge, public bar. *Credit cards:* Amex, Diners, Master, Visa. *Mailing address:* Molesworth Street, Dublin 2. *How to get there:* Molesworth Street is between Dawson Street and Kildare Street. [T]

GEORGIAN HOUSE

> In Dublin . . . the airs of grace and of leisure have not
> departed even if the society which gave them birth is
> past and gone. It is a city of ghosts, but ghosts of the
> so newly dead that something of their earthly presence
> still lingers in the wide streets, the pleasant squares,
> that were their home.
>
> *Honor Tracy, 1956*

Georgian House, built about two hundred years ago by people of society and leisure, is but steps away from St Stephen's Green, largest and
most famous of Dublin squares. Statues of many of the famous "ghosts"
associated with Dublin are set among the beautiful gardens of this park.

The Ante Room Restaurant of Georgian House was successfully
operating before the guest house was opened. It's an attractive place,
with pink cloths layered over white ones, and has become known for
good food at reasonable prices.

A small sitting room is simply furnished. Bedrooms, too, are simply decorated with modern pieces and light colors. Except for those
on the fourth floor (called third floor in Ireland and a bit of a climb),
they are high-ceilinged, and the larger ones have a double and a single
bed instead of twins. All bathrooms have showers. The old coach house
now has five good-size rooms that may be the quietest.

Georgian House is a good value in this very convenient center-city
area.

Price category: Moderate. *Telephone:* (01) 618832. *Rooms:* 15 with
bath, telephone, and TV; ground-floor room. *Meals:* Luncheon and
dinner to public Monday–Saturday; wine license. *Facilities:* Sitting
room, free parking. *Mailing address:* 20 Lower Baggot Street, Dublin
2.   [T]

KILRONAN HOUSE

> The hospitality of Dublin is almost embarrassing to
> an English visitor. . . . There can be no other capital
> in the world more generous in its welcome.
>
> *H. V. Morton*, 1931

An attractive guest house within easy walking distance of a city center
is the sort of lodging travelers all over the world look for. One such
lodging is Kilronan House, which retains some of the graceful atmosphere of the nineteenth century. A crystal chandelier and marble mantel contribute to the old-fashioned air of the little sitting room, as do
cherished old pieces of porcelain in an antique cabinet. The bedrooms
are furnished with a mixture of old and new things, some of them plain.
All have hairdriers, and the ones without private bath have corner
showers. The whole place is immaculate, kept neat and sparkling by
a loyal staff who have stayed on for years. Josephine Murray, then a
young widow, started her guest house in 1962. Visitors return year after year, some spending months at a time. Mrs. Murray makes all her
guests feel like old friends and helps them plan their Dublin visit. She'll
suggest restaurants to which you can walk for dinner.

Kilronan House is two blocks from Saint Stephen's Green, where
you can stroll down the years on paths trod by Oliver Goldsmith, Oscar Wilde, William Butler Yeats, and others of the many literary lu-
minaries produced by Ireland. You could walk a little farther to
twelfth-century Saint Patrick's Cathedral, with its memories of the iras-
cible Dean Jonathan Swift. His tomb in the church is marked by a
plaque, and on a wall is a translation of the Latin epitaph he wrote for
himself, which begins

> Swift has sailed into his rest;
> Savage indignation there
> Cannot lacerate his breast.

Kilronan House has two drawbacks. The stairs to the third and fourth floors (called the second and third floors in Ireland) are steep, and the front bedrooms are noisy all night because of traffic. The latter is not important in winter, when windows are closed; but only the rooms at the back, just one flight up, are recommended for all times of the year.

Price category: Moderate. *Proprietor:* Josephine Murray. *Telephone:* (01) 755266. *Closed:* December 23–31. *Rooms:* 11 with bath, telephone, TV, and tea-making. *Children:* Baby-sitting. *Facilities:* TV room. *Credit cards:* Master, Visa. *Mailing address:* 70 Adelaide Road, Dublin 2. *How to get there:* Adelaide Road is off Lower Leeson Street at the Grand Canal, not far from Saint Stephen's Green.   [T]

SHELBOURNE HOTEL

> The Shelbourne became the scene of so many pleasures that their aroma forever hangs in its air; . . . the place still seems to be thronged with the handsome, the hearty, the happy, and the polite — yesterday's merry ones, to the manner born . . . When lights blaze in the evenings, when morning sunshine comes flashing in from the Green . . . expectation and rapture fill one — *this* is the place! *Elizabeth Bowen,* 1951

The Shelbourne, Dublin's grand hotel, is still *the* place. It began life in 1824 to provide a townhouse for those of the country gentry who did not have their own and to welcome travelers from abroad. William Thackeray was, in 1842, "comfortably accommodated at the . . . daily charge of six-and-eight pence . . . a copious breakfast provided in the coffee-room, a perpetual luncheon likewise there spread, a plentiful dinner ready at six o'clock; after which there is a drawing-room and a rubber of whist, with . . . coffee and cakes in plenty to satisfy the largest appetite."

Rebuilt in 1866, the present Dublin landmark was the setting for much of George Moore's *A Drama in Muslin*, when, "in their snug, firelit Shelbourne rooms, the girls are being decked. . . . All is breathlessness, flutter, and swirls of finery. Up and down the long corridors scurry maids with steaming hot-water cans." Today in those upstairs corridors, stairs go up and down erratically to connect the Victorian building with adjoining Georgian houses and a modern wing.

In the high-ceilinged drawing room whose large windows overlook Saint Stephen's Green, reflected in enormous gilt mirrors dominating each end of the room, Yeats sat reading his poems to his friends. Today the mirrors reflect those coming and going, having tea or a drink, smiling and laughing, meeting friends, or quietly reading.

During the Easter Uprising of 1916, the Shelbourne drew fire from the insurgents encamped on Saint Stephen's Green after British troops, admitted from the rear, garrisoned the hotel. Guests lived in its corridors for a week. In 1922 the constitution of the Irish Free State, precursor of the Irish Republic, was drafted in a sitting room overlooking the green.

More than thirty years ago Elizabeth Bowen wrote, "In this place you never know whom you may not meet. . . . 'Wait now,' says the sociable passer-by, 'till I just have a look and see who is in the Shelbourne!' — and, with a flash of revolving doors, in he whirls, not to be unrewarded. . . . The coffee room rings, and has rung, with grand racy talk. Through the halls flow and have flowed prelates, peers, politicians, sportsmen, tourists, journalists, financiers, athletes, aesthetes, diplomats, debutantes, dramatists, and all the rest of us. In the pageant of figures, the sea of faces, to-day and yesterday merge." Her words still ring true.

Price category: Very expensive. *Manager:* Gerald Lawless. *Telephone:* (01) 766471. *Rooms:* 147 rooms and 19 suites with bath, telephone, and television; suitable for wheelchair guests. *Meals:* Breakfast, luncheon, snacks, tea, dinner for public; full license. *Children:* Babysitting. *Facilities:* Lounge, cocktail bar, gift shop, barber, beauty salon, garage. *Credit cards:* Amex, Carte Blanche, Diners, Master, Visa. *U.S. agent:* THF. *Mailing address:* Saint Stephen's Green, Dublin 2. *How to get there:* Guests can be met at the Dublin airport or railway station. The hotel faces Saint Stephen's Green in the city's center. [T]

Dundalk, Louth

BALLYMASCANLON HOTEL

A garden is a lovesome thing, God wot.
Thomas Edward Brown, 1860

Ballymascanlon, a winner of the National Garden Competition for hotels, is surrounded by 200 acres of gardens and woodlands backed by national forest and mountain scenery. A stream flows through the carefully cultivated flower gardens, and trails wind to an apple orchard, beautiful with bloom in spring; tennis courts are in this setting. A path leads to a 4,000-year-old burial monument, the Proleek dolmen. Science has been unable to explain how the 46-ton capstone was raised onto its three supports.

The hotel's friendly atmosphere starts with the owners, the Quinn family. This is a fine place for anyone who likes to be active, especially good for those traveling with children. An indoor swimming pool, squash courts, gymnasium, sauna, solarium, and billiard room are at the hotel's sports center, where tennis courts are floodlighted at night.

The original part of the hotel was a mansion dating back to the early nineteenth century, where a little of the old atmosphere remains. In an attractive contemporary cellar bar, guests are encouraged to perform in impromptu concerts and singsongs. Care is taken in the preparation of every meal, and all vegetables are grown in the gardens.

Ballymascanlon is associated with one of Ireland's tragic episodes. It was once the home of Count Plunket, father of Joseph Mary Plunket, one of the "martyrs of 1916" who were shot after their surrender in the uprising that eventually led to Ireland's freedom. Wherever one goes in Ireland, history is close at hand.

Price category: Moderate. *Proprietors:* Brian and Oliver Quinn. *Telephone:* (042) 71124. *Closed:* Christmas. *Rooms:* 38 with bath, telephone, TV, and tea-making. *Meals:* Luncheon, snacks, tea, supper, dinner for public; full license. *Children:* Baby-sitting and -listening; playground. *Facilities:* 3 lounges, TV room, cocktail bar, garden. *Activities:* Indoor pool, floodlighted tennis, squash, sauna, gym, solarium, and billiards at the hotel; ocean swimming, riding, and trout and salmon fishing nearby. *Credit cards:* Amex, Diners, Master, Visa. *U.S. agent:* Best Western. *How to get there:* The hotel is on Route N1, 3 miles north of Dundalk.   [T]

RATHSALLAGH HOUSE

> If you are fortunate enough to be bidden to the right
> houses in Ireland to-day, you will have as much good
> talk as you are likely to hear in any other place in this
> degenerate age, which has mostly forgotten how to
> converse. . . .
>
> *Kate Douglas Wiggin,* 1900

You'll be bound to converse with your hosts and the other guests at this gracious, informal home. All is friendliness here. The original Rathsallagh House burned in 1798. The stables were then converted to make this attractive lodging that is somewhat off the beaten track.

The house is decorated as you'd expect a fine country house to be — with big comfortable chairs in front of log fires, Oriental rugs, antique furniture, floral chintz in light, lovely colors, oil paintings, plants and fresh flowers. In the dining room, white flowered chintz draperies are set off against red walls. Bedrooms vary in size, two on the small side, as do the bathrooms, some very large. Most have showers and are warmly carpeted.

Dinner is a sumptuous set meal with choices. The three starters might include cheese soufflé, avocado and bacon salad or Rathsallagh seafood. Next comes a soup, then a sorbet. The main course could be fillet of beef with horseradish sauce, black sole with fennel, or Wicklow spring lamb, followed by a choice of desserts such as strawberry shortcake, homemade ice cream or trifle. A cheese board follows.

Lawns and gardens surround the house, which is on an estate of 500 acres. It's a place to relax for several days. We hated to leave.

Price category: Expensive. *Proprietors:* Kay and Joe O'Flynn. *Telephone:* (045) 53112. *Closed:* One week at Christmas. *Rooms:* 10 with bath, telephone, and tea-making. 2 ground-floor rooms; suitable for wheel chair guests. *Meals:* Dinner to public by reservation; wine license. *Children:* Under 12 not permitted. *Facilities:* Drawing room, billiard room, garden. *Activities:* Indoor pool, tennis, sauna, and clay pigeon shooting at the house; hunting nearby. *Credit cards:* Diners, Master,

Visa. *U.S. agent:* Robert Reid *How to get there:* From Dunlavin go south on the road to Grange Con. Rathsallagh is about 2 miles along on the left.   [T]

We appreciate hearing about your experiences. If you have comments, suggestions, or recommendations about these or other inns, please use the Reader Report form at the back of this book, or write to us directly: Eileen and Eugene O'Reilly, P.O. Box 484F, Newport, Rhode Island 02840 U.S.A. Your comments are valuable to us.

OLD GROUND HOTEL

> I shall be very happy if these pages shall be able to
> awaken in one bosom . . . the desire to travel towards
> Ireland next year.
>
> *William Makepeace Thackeray,* 1842

For many long-time travelers to Ireland, the Old Ground is the first
stop, since it is only 12 miles from Shannon Airport. The ivy-covered
stone building is in the center of Ennis, behind a broad lawn where
garden furniture is set out. Public rooms are attractive, with some good
antiques among the well-maintained furnishings. Some bedrooms were
much better than others when we last saw them. Refurbishing was going
on, but it would be good to ask to see available rooms when you arrive.

After a rest from your flight you can walk around this good-sized
town, browsing through its many stores to get a start on your shopping. Or you can drive west to the coast, where you will see donkeys
in tiny fields enclosed by stone walls and scattered along a landscape
of rock. Over the centuries these fields have been made by humans who
laboriously hauled seaweed from the Atlantic and spread it over small
patches of dirt. First the patches had to be cleared of rocks by building the walls. Earth was so precious that neighbors were known to take
each other to law for removing earth in baskets from one another's land.
Viewing this patchwork of rock slabs and little clearings threaded by
stone walls will give you the feeling of being in a foreign country.

Although less personal than an owner-run guest house, the atmosphere at this member of the Trust House Forte chain is friendly. You
might even make new friends over a cup of tea set before a cheerful
fire in the lounge or in the intimate Poet's Corner bar. If your taste is
for a hotel of many services — such as direct-dial telephones in
bedrooms — the Old Ground is a good choice.

Price category: Expensive. *Manager:* Kieran Greenway. *Telephone:*
(065) 28127. *Rooms:* 60 with bath, TV, and telephone; suitable for
wheelchair guests. *Meals:* Luncheon, snacks, tea, dinner for public;
full license. *Children:* Baby-sitting, children's meals. *Facilities:* Lounge,
sitting room, cocktail bar, garden. *Activities:* Tennis, indoor pool,
squash, and sauna nearby. *Credit cards:* Amex, Diners, Master, Visa.
U.S. agent: THF. *How to get there:* Ennis is on Route N18, about 12
miles north of Shannon airport.   [T]

SMYTH'S VILLAGE HOTEL

> Where glows the Irish hearth with peat
> There gives a subtle spell —
> The faint blue smoke, the gentle heat,
> The moorland odours tell.
>
> *T.W. Rolleston*

This small modern hotel is different from any other in Ireland. Its straightforward white plaster exterior harmonizes with whitewashed Irish farm cottages. The simple but handsome rustic decor features natural Irish materials: sugan chairs, woven Irish wool spreads. Liscannor stone floors.

A great stone fireplace in the bar glows from a peat fire; the room is lit by the soft flicker of oil lamps; antique platters embellish rough plaster walls. Under the vaulted ceiling you might hear spontaneous music played on Irish instruments or join in singing Irish ballads. The dining room has bare wood tables with red, Irish-wool place mats that match the draperies. Bedrooms are compact, except for four that are family rooms with four beds each. Antique accents such as clocks, lamps, and china are used throughout. The effect is warm and hospitable.

Cottages built as part of the Irish Rent-a-Cottage home scheme are across the road. Vacationers in these enjoy joining the camaraderie at Smyth's Village Hotel bar. From here it's an easy drive to Coole Park, once the home of Lady Gregory and now a forest park, then on to Thoor Ballylee, the Noman tower home of W.B. Yeats. The hotel is only 20 miles from Shannon airport and gives wonderful value. There is a large reduction for a stay of two or more nights.

Price category: Very inexpensive. *Proprietors:* Con and Margaret Smyth. *Telephone:* (0619) 24002. *Closed:* November through March. *Rooms:* 12 with bath; ground-floor rooms. *Meals:* Snacks, and dinner for public; full license. *Children:* Baby-sitting. *Facilities:* TV lounge, cocktail bar, writing room, garden. *Activities:* Tennis at the hotel; boat rental, boat trips on the Shannon, coarse and game fishing, and lake swimming nearby. *How to get there:* From Shannon Airport, drive 20 miles to Feakle via Six-Mile-Bridge and Kilkishen.   [T]

Ferns, Wexford

CLONE HOUSE

> Have you become a farmer? Is it not pleasanter than
> to be shut up within 4 walls and delving eternally with
> a pen? . . . if you are half as much delighted with the
> farm as I am, you bless your stars.
>
> *Thomas Jefferson*

Homespun friendliness is the rule at the seventeenth-century Clone
House, the winner of the national award in 1988 for the best farm guest
house. Wexford is one of the more prosperous parts of Ireland, and
farms such as this have been well kept. Entrance to the landscaped
grounds, which have twice won the National Garden Award for farm-
houses, is through an Old World stone arch. An antique iron foot
scraper in the form of a lion guards the doorway to a house built in
1640. The comfortably furnished rooms hold some fine things from
past generations—old hunting prints, an Empire drop-leaf table, a brass
bed, and a cheval glass among them. In a bay-windowed dining room,
Chippendale chairs surround a mahogany table. Silver and cut glass
are displayed. Almost all of the food served here is produced on the
farm.

Fishermen, or would-be fishermen, can try their luck in a trout
stream that flows through the farm's almost 300 acres. Ferns was the
capital of the ancient Kingdom of Leinster. It holds the remains of a
thirteenth-century castle, perhaps the finest of its kind in Ireland, as
well as an Augustinian abbey and a cathedral.

Price category: Very inexpensive. *Proprietor:* Betty Breen. *Telephone:* (054) 66113. *Closed:* November through February. *Rooms:* 5,
3 with bath. *Meals:* Dinner for the public by reservation; wine license.
Children: Baby-sitting; playground. *Facilities:* Living room, TV room,
garden, and laundry. *Activities:* Fishing and river swimming on the
farm; ocean swimming, outdoor pool, tennis, squash, boat rental, deep-
sea fishing, riding, and hunting nearby. *How to get there:* Clone House
is signposted on Route N11, 2 miles southeast of Ferns.

Foulksmills, Wexford

HORETOWN HOUSE

The horses snort to be at the sport,
The dogs are running free
The woods rejoice at the merry noise
Of Hey tantara tee ree!

William Gray, 1530

A combination of unsurpassed hospitality, congenial people, great home-cooking, and a riding school registered with Bord na gCapall, the Irish Horse Board, makes this one of the outstanding farmhouse lodgings in all Ireland.

The school is run by David, a son of the house, and his American wife, Sarah, both certified instructors. Experienced horsemen can ride through country lanes, try the cross-country course, take part in the gymkhanas held all summer, or join a hunt almost every day of the week in season. There is an eighteenth-century stable yard with box stalls, a paddock for instruction and jumping, and an indoor riding ring. Children and beginners can sign up for group or individual instruction. Best of all, travelers whose children get bored touring can leave them at Horetown House for a course of instruction, secure in the knowledge that they will be taken care of while the parents continue through the rest of Ireland or even the rest of Europe.

The house, an early-eighteenth-century farm manor set on 214 acres, is enjoyed by travelers regardless of the degree of their interest in horses. In the lounge, around a huge log fire, guests are introduced to each other and made to feel at home immediately. Some good antique furnishings are mixed with many that are time-worn.

Guests have a choice between dinner in the dining room or in the Cellar Restaurant, open to the public and convenient for those arriving late (perhaps from the nearby ferry from Wales). The restaurant is in a high-ceilinged, vaulted area where dozens of servants once held sway in this former "upstairs-downstairs" house.

A visitor wrote in the guest book, "The door an open heart to all who enter."

Price category: Very inexpensive. *Proprietors:* Vera and Theo Young. *Telephone:* (051) 63633. *Closed:* January 10 through March 10 except by reservation. *Rooms:* 12 with shared baths. *Meals:* Snacks, tea and dinner for guests; dinner for public by reservation (except Sunday and Monday from September through June); wine license. *Children:* Playground, table tennis, riding instruction. *Facilities:* Drawing room, TV lounge, garden. *Activities:* Riding and hunting at the house; ocean swimming, fishing, windsurfing, and boat rental nearby. *How to get there:* The house is between Foulksmills and Taghmon. A taxi can meet guests at the Wexford railway station.   [T]

ARDILAUN HOUSE HOTEL

> Gentlemen's seats, on the road from Galway to Moy-
> cullen, are scattered in great profusion.
> *William Makepeace Thackeray*, 1842

Once a "gentleman's seat" on the road out of Galway, Ardilaun House
is now a large hotel in a part of town called Salthill, about ten minutes
away from the center. A bus goes by the entrance gate.

There is still something of the country-house feeling about Ardilaun.
The staff is exceptionally helpful and friendly for such a large hotel.
Open fires burn in lounges that are furnished with chintz and velvet-
covered chairs in light colors; bedrooms have matching floral wallpaper,
spreads, and draperies. Sometimes there is dancing in an attractive
beamed dining room, where food is consistently good.

While Ardilaun—isolated in extensive grounds that are a haven of
peace and beauty—has a refined air, Salthill is a holiday suburb with
many of the honky-tonk aspects of busy seaside resorts. You'll find a
walk to the beach from the hotel an interesting look at a slice of Irish
life the casual visitor to Ireland may miss. Galway is a historic city that
owes its existence to the sea. Spanish galleons were once a common sight
in its harbor, from which you can take a boat to the primitive Aran
Islands. A shorter boat trip is to go by waterbus up the river into Lough
Corrib. In season there is a conducted walking tour of the city each
evening.

Price category: Moderate. *Manager:* Tom McCarthy-O'Hea. *Telephone:* (091) 21433. *Rooms:* 90, and 6 suites, with bath, TV, and telephone. Elevator. *Meals:* Luncheon, snacks, tea, dinner for public; full
license. *Children:* Baby-sitting. *Facilities:* 3 lounges, cocktail bar, garden. *Activities:* Ocean swimming, tennis, pitch and putt, deep-sea fishing, boat rental, boat trips, and riding nearby. *Credit cards:* Amex,
Diners, Master, Visa. *How to get there:* Follow signs from Galway to
Salthill. Turn right at O'Flaherty's garage onto Taylor's Hill. The hotel
is signposted about a mile farther on.   [T]

GREAT SOUTHERN HOTEL

> The people of Galway are very proud of being from
> Galway, though, personally, I think it is silly enough
> being proud of being from anywhere in particular.
> *Brendan Behan,* 1962

The people of Galway are very proud of their grand old Great Southern Hotel. Built in 1845, its opening coincided with the inauguration of a packet service between Galway and St John's, Newfoundland. It has reigned as the leading hostelry of Galway ever since, the center of social life and the place visiting dignitaries stay. Today it is a handsome mix of Old-World charm and contemporary luxury.

Serene soft colors decorate public rooms; a high-ceilinged lobby--lounge retains a splendid original fireplace of Connemara marble. Ask for a bedroom in the original building. Recommended in food guides, the restaurant offers such specialities as sea food right from Galway's fishing boats. The friendly Old Railway Bar, where you may join townspeople for a drink or a chat, is an oasis after a day spent exploring wild Connemara. Frequent evening entertainment features local artists in a cabaret called Taste of Galway. A public car park is 200 yards away, but parking can be difficult.

The hotel faces Eyre Square, the town green, where there is a memorial garden for President John F. Kennedy who spoke there. From it you can walk to shops and to most places in town you'll want to see.

Price category: Very expensive. *Manager:* Terry Brennan. *Telephone:* (091) 64041. *Rooms:* 115 with bath, TV, and telephone; 6 suites; elevator. *Meals:* Luncheon, snacks, tea, dinner for public; full license. *Children:* Baby-sitting. *Facilities:* Lounge, cocktail bar, public bar, hair salon, craft shop. *Activities:* Indoor pool, gym, sauna, and musical entertainment at hotel; water-skiing, windsurfing, scuba diving, boat rental, boat or plane trips to the Aran Islands, and deep-sea fishing nearby. *Credit cards:* Amex, Diners, Master, Visa. *U.S. agent:* CIE Tours. *How to get there:* The hotel is in the center of town facing the green. [T]

MARINE HOTEL

Of all the gems which deck our isle
And stud our native shore
None wears for me a sunny smile
As bright as sweet Glandore.

Dr Morris, 1860

Boats bob at anchor right in front of the Marine Hotel, which is just across a narrow road from an enchanting bay on the beautiful west Cork coast. Owned by the O'Brien family since 1910, the hotel has grown with each generation. You'll receive a warm welcome from Sean and Teresa, the present owners.

Furnishings are modern and comfortable. A feature not found in many of our recommendations is the large bar-lounge where Irish ballad sessions are held each weekend in summer and sometimes midweek as well. If you are an early-to-bed person, you won't be disturbed if you ask for a bedroom at the other end of the hotel. An attractive dining room, with a window wall that faces the water, specializes in steak and seafood prepared under the direction of chef Sean.

The hotel angling boat, with skipper, can be hired to explore the estuaries, coves, and harbors teeming with mackerel, bass, pollock, and more. Sandy beaches are within easy reach, and Glandore harbor is ideal for small boating, sailing, and windsurfing.

A long time ago, author Jonathan Swift wrote a poem, in Latin, about the beauty of Glandore. Originally a fishing port, Glandore is now better known as a holiday village and a port of call for yachtsmen on the westward run from Kinsale. Unspoiled and uncommercialized, it has a special appeal.

Price category: Moderate. *Proprietors:* Sean and Teresa O'Brien. *Telephone:* (028) 33366. *Closed:* October through March. *Rooms:* 16 with bath and TV. *Meals:* Luncheon, snacks, dinner for public; full license. *Children:* Baby-sitting, playroom. *Facilities:* Lounge, bar--lounge, public bar, game room. *Activities:* Sail boat, outboard, and canoe rental, ocean swimming, shore and boat fishing, and riding near-by. *Credit cards:* Master, Visa. *U.S. agent:* RS. *How to get there:* Glandore is on the shore in west Cork, 4 miles west of Rosscarbery. [T]

AHERLOW HOUSE HOTEL

> Up the airy mountain,
> Down the rushy glen,
> We daren't go a-hunting
> For fear of little men;
> Wee folk, good folk,
> Trooping all together;
> Green jacket, red cap,
> And a white owl's feather!
>
> *William Allingham,* 1874

We don't know if you'll see any leprechauns in this bewitching glen, or their pots of gold, but you will find an attractive hotel called Aherlow House, set in a woods echoing with the sound of streams.

A large bar-lounge with a terrific view has chairs arranged around a big fireplace. A sitting room with the same view is attractively furnished with some antiques. Old prints decorate walls. Ask to see which of the nicely-decorated bedrooms are available when you arrive, as some are larger than others and, not all have a view. This recently refurbished hotel has reopened under new owners.

Price category: Inexpensive. *Manager:* Austin Gleeson. *Telephone:* (062) 56147. *Rooms:* 10 with bath, telephone, and TV; ground floor rooms; weekend breaks. *Meals:* Luncheon in high season only; snacks, tea, dinner to public; full license. *Children:* Baby-sitting. *Facilities:* Living room, cocktail lounge, garden. *Activities:* Indoor pool, squash, sauna, and riding nearby. *How to get there:* The hotel in on a minor road 6 miles south of Tipperary town. Turn west off Route N24 at Bansha.

[T]

GLENCAR HOTEL

> By a stone causeway across the bog you walk up
> through holly thickets and copses where London Pride
> grows wild, to the little Glencar Hotel in the wilds,
> which has been visited by everybody who ever really
> knew Ireland.
>
> *Stephen Gwynn*, 1927

In the mountainous Kerry southwest there is a hotel that is remote even in this sparsely populated county. Far from the tourist routes, generations of Dalys have played host to fishermen, writers, and those simply seeking peace and solitude. Once a sporting lodge of the Lansdowne family, this has been one of Ireland's premier fishing hotels for nearly a hundred years. The Dalys own miles of fishing rights on rivers and lakes. Macgillycuddy's Reeks rise in the east, cloud-wreathed Carrantuohill towering over all. The glen is full of changing light and color peculiar to the west of Ireland. Wild hawthorne, blue hyacinths, and primroses color the green meadows and climb rocky rises. In autumn the red berries of the rowan tree glow along the roadsides.

In May we drove down a half-mile driveway lined with rhododendron in bloom. We entered Glencar Hotel through a sunporch where fishermen had parked waders and creels and where a rack on the wall held fishing rods. Inside, the atmosphere was homey—or homely, to use the Irish word for it. (If you hear something in Ireland or Britain called homely, don't expect to find it unattractive.) Gazing happily at the panorama outside, we enjoyed tea in a sun lounge. At the other end of the room some guests were playing pool. A dart board hung on a wall; playing cards and chess were on a table. In a large living room there were good books and magazines, and chairs to curl up in away from the television, which had a room to itself. Fishermen swapped stories before dinner in a congenial bar. When Brendan Behan ended up here years ago while roistering with some Kerry friends, the quiet bar resounded to a more convivial evening than it had been used to.

The furnishings of the hotel are quite a mix—good Sheraton and Queen Anne antiques, Victoriana, and some hotel-modern. The walls are well covered with hunting-lodge antlers, oil paintings in heavy gold frames, photographs of former guests with their abundant catches, hunting and shooting prints, and contemporary paintings of the superlative Kerry scenery. All this is tossed together with an excess of pattern, but the whole thing comes off snug—especially when you sit beside a log fire with the wind rumbling outside. Bedrooms are plain. In the dining room a limited menu offers standard fare, but the sunset views from the large windows are worth the trip.

Salmon fishing here lures sportsmen from around the world. From February through June, when the fishing is best, 90 percent of the guests are Continental, predominently German. When the renowned Irish writer Seán O'Faoláin stayed at Glencar, he wrote that he was filled with excitement at the thought that he was penetrating into one of Ireland's loneliest places and at the sight of the wilderness, and he hated to leave it. You may hate to leave too. In the tiny village of Glencar you can dance at a *ceilidh* on Sundays in summer or join a singsong at the little Climber's Inn.

Price category: Inexpensive to moderate. *Proprietor:* Karl Daly. *Telephone:* (066) 60102. *Closed:* Mid-October through January. *Rooms:* 30, 14 with bath; ground-floor rooms. *Meals:* Dinner for guests; full license. *Children:* Baby-sitting. *Facilities:* Lounge, TV lounge, sun parlor, cocktail bar, garden. *Activities:* Trout and salmon fishing, tennis, and boat rental at the hotel; ocean swimming and riding nearby. *Credit card:* Amex. *How to get there:* Glencar is signposted in Killorglin and at many points around the Ring of Kerry. It is on the road that encircles Lake Caragh.   [T]

GLIN CASTLE

> The lofty hall, staircases, galleries,
> And rooms of State; should I undertake
> To show what 'tis doth them so glorious make,
> The pictures, sculptures, carving, graving, gilding,
> Twould be as long in writing, as in building.
> *Charles Cotton*

Live as a lord at Glin Castle, the home of the Knight of Glin. He is a descendant of a branch of the great FitzGerald family, who arrived with the Anglo-Norman invasion and have owned this property since the thirteenth century. They once owned a great barony here defended by more than a dozen medieval castles. A fragment of one survives in Glin village, and in 1600 it was one of the last strongholds to stand siege in the war against Queen Elizabeth's English forces. Other descendants of the FitzGeralds' owned baronies all over Ireland, but Glin Castle and its estate is the only surviving property still held by the family.

The present castle, dating from the eighteenth century, contains an impressive collection of antiques including elaborately carved mahogany chairs, graceful tables in all shapes, breakfront bookcases, desks, and Oriental rugs. Young Madam Olda FitzGerald, a writer, describes it as "a house that has gradually grown together, room by room, generation by generation, until it has become a living page out of the history of Irish craftsmen." Its double-flying staircase is unique in Ireland, and there is only one other like it in all the British Isles. Rococo plasterwork ceilings are of fine quality, and although the walls are covered with oil paintings—of people, dogs, horses, buildings, landscapes, and seascapes—there is still room for elaborately framed mirrors, handsome sconces, china, and old prints. Swords and maps, antique musical instruments, and mounted stags' heads recall generations of activity.

There are various ways you can stay at Glin Castle. The FitzGeralds live in one wing. You can rent the main castle, with a staff of a cook and two housekeepers, for the whole summer season. At other times

it is for rent by the week, fortnight, or month. But you can arrange to stay in the main castle for one or more nights as a paying guest of the Knight and Madam FitzGerald, who will dine with you and guide you through its treasures. They are friendly and informal. (She was in jeans the morning we arrived.) The Knight, a writer and art historian, is the representative in Ireland for Christie's international auction house. He also farms the estate. There are a gift shop and tea room, open to the public, in a gate lodge.

You could live out a fantasy and have the place to yourself—even for a night—to experience what life would be like in your own castle with a staff to keep you comfortable and well fed. If you want to gather all generations of your family together for a house party, there is a sunny nursery complete with doll houses, toy forts, and teddy bears. Bedrooms with chintz-covered beds and chaises are decorated with Victorian painted-china wash sets (although piping hot water now flows into bathrooms that have fluffy white towels on heated towel bars). The castle can be made warm even in coldest weather. It is a true home, and the staff are family retainers. Olda FitzGerald wrote, "Sometimes, standing here with my hand on the smooth inlaid wood of the stair-rail in the immense peace of this great house, I feel that if ever I'm to see a ghost, it must be now. But it never is, and there is only the tapping of the roses on the windowpane, and the soughing of the great Pinus Insignus dropping its pine needles gently on to whichever pram is underneath it on the lawn below."

Arrangements must be made through the FitzGeralds' Dublin agent (listed below), not directly with the castle. This is a good location for golfers who want to play the famous courses at Ballybunion, Tralee, and Killarney. To stay here is a romantic experience, and those who delight in beautiful surroundings shouldn't miss it.

Price category: Very expensive. *Proprietors:* The Knight of Glin and Madam FitzGerald. *Agent's telephone:* (01) 751665. *Rooms:* Suites with dressing rooms and bath for a total of 13 guests. *Meals:* All meals for guests; full license. *Children:* Baby-sitting, nursery playroom. *Facilities:* Drawing room, library, smoking room, garden room, garden, gift shop. *Activities:* Tennis at the house. *Mailing address of agent:* Elegant Ireland, 15 Harcourt Street, Dublin 2, Ireland. *How to get there:* Glin is on the south shore of the Shannon estuary, just east of the Tarbert-ferry landing, on Route N69.

MARLFIELD HOUSE

> I am . . . delighted with all I have seen, the mere wood,
> water and wilderness are intermingled with an appear-
> ance of fertility which never accompanies them in our
> land, and with a brilliancy of verdure which justifies
> your favorite epithet of the green isle.
>
> *Sir Walter Scott*, 1825

When Sir Walter wrote the words above to his friend, author Maria
Edgeworth, Marlfield House was the dower house for the residence of
the earl of Courtown, on an estate encompassing 17,000 acres. Today
it is one of the outstanding country-house hotels in Ireland.

Period elegance and modern comfort are well combined here.
Rooms are furnished with antiques chosen as if for a private home. A
half-tester bed hung with flowered chintz dominated our bedroom. We
were intrigued with a double Waterford chandelier whose chain hung
from a plaster medallion on the third-floor ceiling down through the
open well of a sweeping staircase. There was a chandelier at the second-floor level and another in the first-floor entrance hall. The hotel
is luxuriously carpeted throughout.

The large drawing room, hung with another Waterford chandelier,
has chairs upholstered with cut velvet, flowered linen draperies that
are expertly swagged, a grand piano, and a bar at one end. When we
lingered over tea on a Sunday afternoon, a group of Irish guests from
the neighborhood were enjoying their Guinness while playing a quiet
game of cards. The atmosphere is refined but not stuffy.

The cuisine, which has won enthusiastic recommendations in restaurant guides, became so popular that more dining space was needed. Mary Bowe is not one to have her period house spoiled by an
ordinary modern extension. She commissioned architects to design an
imaginative domed conservatory that opens onto colorful gardens behind the house. Classic country meals served at Marlfield House feature coquilles Saint Jacques, grilled turbot meunière, sole Colbert, and
sea trout; and there are always roasts. If you stop for a light lunch, you'll

find such dishes as crab salad, omelets, and soused herring, as well as soups and sandwiches.

Sandy beaches are only 2 miles away. Marlfield House owes its charm to the taste, skill, and personality of its owner, Mary Bowe, who is to be commended for this outstanding addition to Ireland's country inns.

Price category: Very expensive. *Proprietor:* Mary Bowe. *Telephone:* (055) 21124. *Closed:* Christmas. *Rooms:* 13 with bath, telephone, and TV; 6 suites. Reservation for two days required weekends. *Meals:* Luncheon, snacks, tea, and dinner for public; full license. *Children:* Not suitable for those under six. *Facilities:* Drawing room, library, cocktail bar, garden, antique and craft shop. *Activities:* Tennis at the house; ocean swimming, deep-sea and freshwater fishing, riding, and hunting nearby. *U.S. agent:* Robert Reid Associates. *How to get there:* The hotel is on Route R742 east of Gorey. Guests can be met at the Gorey railway station. [T]

PARKSTOWN HOUSE

> O, the hills, the hills so green
> May heaven shine o'er them ever sheen
> The hills of sweet Tipperary.
>
> *Robert Joyce*

Drive through black-and-white entrance gates, down a long driveway through beautifully kept grounds, to this Georgian mansion built in 1770. Horses graze in the fields, which seems appropriate in a place called Horse and Jockey.

The interior of the house matches the inviting quality of the exterior. Among furnishings we noted were chairs covered in velvet and leather, a marble-topped gilt console, a display of silver and Waterford glass, an elaborate brass chandelier, marble mantels, guns and swords hung on a wall, Victorian armoires, and sheepskin rugs. There is nothing here of faded glory; everything is in fine condition.

Only the bathrooms have a late twentieth-century look. The double bedrooms that share baths are much larger than the one that has a private bath. Guests meet each other around the large Hepplewhite table in the dining room and before a peat and log fire in the drawing room.

If you drive from Parkstown House to see the Rock of Cashel, you will be on the best approach to get your first glimpse of the famous ruins. As you come in from the north, you see them high above the town, silhouetted against the sky, a striking scene.

Price category: Very inexpensive. *Proprietor:* Mrs. Ena Maher. *Telephone:* (0504) 44315. *Closed:* October through March. *Rooms:* 5, 1 with bath. *Meals:* Dinner for guests; no license. *Facilities:* Drawing room, TV room, garden. *Activities:* Tennis and riding nearby. *How to get there:* The house is on the main Dublin–Cork road, Route N8, 7 miles north of Cashel.

CULLINTRA HOUSE

> It is always pleasant to arrive in Ireland. There is a
> certain softness in the air . . . as though it were robed
> in a delicate dress made out of threads of rain and a
> myriad dewdrops, woven together by magic.
>
> *Lord Dunsany,* 1937

It is always pleasant to arrive at Cullintra House, where a log fire in the hearth keeps the living room cozy all winter. Comfortable tufted chairs, some upholstered in green velvet, are beside antique tables that hold interesting magazines.

Candles lend a soft glow to the dining room, where the food is exceptionally good, and even those who arrive late will be served if they telephone. They might have a first course of prawn cocktail, smoked salmon, or pâté, followed by homemade soup. Roast beef or a chicken casserole could be the entrée, topped off by a home-baked pie.

Patricia Cantlon raises beef cattle and sheep. This 200-year-old house is near Kilkenny, a medieval city with narrow lanes, a Norman castle (open to the public), and two monasteries in use since the thirteenth century. County Kilkenny has the greatest concentration of craft workers in Ireland.

Price category: Very inexpensive. *Proprietor:* Patricia Cantlon. *Telephone:* (051) 23614. *Rooms:* 5 sharing baths. *Meals:* Dinner for public by reservation; no license. *Children:* Baby-sitting. *Facilities:* Living room, conservatory, garden. *Activities:* River and ocean swimming, tennis, coarse fishing, and indoor pool nearby. *Mailing address:* The Rower, Inistioge, County Kilkenny. *How to get there:* The house is 6 miles from New Ross on the Kilkenny road.

Kanturk, Cork

ASSOLAS COUNTRY HOUSE

> There is no country in this world so pleasant for stran-
> gers; while so abundant is the recompense of enjoy-
> ment it can supply, that for every new visitor it receives,
> it will obtain a new friend.
>
> *Mr. and Mrs. S.C. Hall,* 1835

There is probably no guest house more pleasant for strangers than Assolas House. Every visitor will become a new friend who will be eager
to return. Guests assemble for sherry in the spacious drawing room before a dinner served from family silver. Log fires add to the welcoming atmosphere. Fruit and fresh vegetables used in home-cooked meals
are from the gardens. After-dinner coffee in the drawing room, well
mannered but informal, adds to the feeling of being in a private house
where guests mingle cordially.

Bedrooms are large and furnished in casual country style with floral fabrics and antiques. The gardens have won the prized National Gardens Competition award for guest houses. A well-maintained grass tennis court should prove an interesting novelty for most American tennis players, and there are boats to row on the farm's own lake.

Walking from one section of Assolas to another is a tour through the centuries. The date and origin of the Jacobean section is clouded in the mists of time, but it was probably a monastery until they were banned under Queen Elizabeth I. Irish troops were billeted here in the mid-seventeenth century, and to this day there's a wood called the "Soldiers' Grave" where casualties of their cavalry skirmishes were buried. A wing was built a hundred years later, and the final addition is in the Queen Anne style of the early eighteenth century. The fresco around the hall ceiling and the carved doors are the work of skilled craftsmen, while most of the windowpanes of the house are the original wavy handblown glass.

A minister once lived here who, every night for thirty-four years, hung a lantern high on the walls of Assolas, shining its welcome light on the nearby waters of a ford to guide the traveler on his way. Many a life was saved from the swollen river and from the hands of highway gangs lurking at dangerous crossings. His house was always open, in true Irish fashion, to receive the wounded should they fall prey to the roaming bands. The house by the ford became known in Gaelic as Ata Solus, meaning the "ford of the light." The anglicized version is Assolas, a place that captures the essence of Irish country-house living.

Price category: Expensive to very expensive. *Proprietors:* The Bourke Family. *Telephone:* (029) 50015. *Closed:* November to mid-March. *Rooms:* 10 with bath and telephone. *Meals:* Snacks, tea, and supper for guests, dinner for public by reservation; full license. *Facilities:* Drawing room, TV room, garden. *Activities:* Tennis and rowing at the house; riding and free golf nearby. *U.S. agent:* Robert Reid Associates. *How to get there:* The house is signposted on Route N72, the Mallow-Killarney road. Do *not* go into Kanturk. Guests can be met at the Shannon or Cork airport or at the Mallow railway station.[T]

Kenmare, Kerry

HAWTHORNE HOUSE

> The gentlemen and inhabitants of this county are all
> of them remarkable for their hospitality to strangers.
> *Dr. Smith,* 1750

At Hawthorne House you'll find the same hospitality to strangers that Dr. Smith found in Kerry over two hundred years ago. Although it is the home of Ann and Gerry Brown, this particularly nice guest house has been recently remodeled to seem almost like a small hotel.

Hawthorne House is attractively decorated, with a pleasant little sitting room where guests can order a glass of wine while they exchange travel experiences before they go out for dinner. Ann can recommend a variety of restaurants in the town. Fruit and flowers welcome guests in bedrooms. The more expensive ones have sitting areas and TV.

Here you'll have the advantage of being in a town that is large enough to have good shopping but small enough to cover on foot. The house is on a side street, just a little away from the busy center. Be sure to indulge yourself with a drink or afternoon tea at the Park Hotel.

Kerry can be surprisingly mild in winter, when Hawthorne House is open and most lodgings are closed. It's a real bargain.

Price category: Very inexpensive. *Proprietors:* Ann and Gerry Browne. *Telephone:* (064) 41035. *Rooms:* 7 with bath, some with TV. *Facilities:* Sitting room, garden. *Activities:* Golf, ocean swimming, wind-surfing, scuba diving, snorkling, boat trips, deep-sea fishing, and riding nearby. *How to get there:* The house is on Shelbourne Street almost beside the main entrance to the Park Hotel.

Kenmare, Kerry

PARK HOTEL

> The south-western part of Kerry is now well known
> as the most beautiful tract in the British Isles.
> *Thomas Babington Macauley,* 1844

If you are looking for the very best of luxury hotels, and you prefer
a stately old one to a glossy new one, you need look no further. The
Park, a Victorian dowager once in the Great Southern hotel chain, has
been restored beyond its original grandeur. It has one of the most im-

pressive arrays of antiques of any hotel in Ireland, and, though in the busy town of Kenmare, stands in 11 acres of parkland and tropical foliage. A five-minute walk takes you to a lively harbor offering all sorts of water activities. Kenmare is a center for such scenic wonders as Killarney, Glengarriff, Healy Pass, Gougane Barra, and the Ring of Kerry, all only a short drive away.

Public rooms at the Park are warm and elegant. Reception is at an early Georgian partners' desk. One conversation piece, an ancient painted Italian rainwater receptacle bought at Harrods, took eleven men to install it in the entrance lounge. Soft pastel colors harmonize with the furnishings; elaborate draperies may be swagged, padded, or topped with gilt cornices. Even the wide bedroom corridors are lavishly furnished with oil paintings and antiques. Some bedrooms hold draped four-posters.

Items of classic French cuisine are a specialty in an award-winning dining room that overlooks terraced lawns to the bay beyond. Lobster and other seafood are fresh from the Atlantic. The Park's friendliness and informality, rare at large luxury hotels, are no doubt due to its jovial young proprietor. Francis Brennan is always about, chatting with his guests. Your only difficulty in staying here will be to leave. Although the hotel closes in mid-November, it reopens for gala Christmas and New Year's programs.

Price category: Very expensive. *Telephone:* (064) 41200. *Proprietor:* Francis Brennan. *Closed:* Mid-November through March, except December 22-January 2. *Rooms:* 44 with bath and telephone. Elevator. Christmas and New Year's programs. *Meals:* Snacks, tea, dinner for public; full license. *Facilities:* Lounge, TV lounge, cocktail bar, garden. *Activities:* Golf at the hotel; ocean swimming, wind-surfing, snorkeling, scuba diving, deep-sea fishing, and riding nearby. *Credit cards:* Diners, Master, Visa. *U.S. agent:* Selective Hotels. *How to get there:* Kenmare is on Route N71, between Bantry and Killarney. The hotel will arrange limousine service from Shannon airport and a car with driver for day trips.   [T]

AGHADOE HEIGHTS HOTEL

> We would travel the green hills and mountains,
> By the road to the Gap of Dunloe,
> And along by the Glens and the Valleys,
> To a spot that is called Aghadoe.
>
> *J. M. Crofts*

The Irish tradition of hospitality is a reality at Aghadoe Heights, even though the hotel is fairly large and completely modern. Its hilltop setting affords what is probably the most comprehensive view of the Killarney district, with a panorama of the fabled lakes backed by purple mountains. Ask for a bedroom facing this scenic grandeur. The rooftop dining room, with a reputation for good food, takes advantage of the same view.

The decor is vivacious, the atmosphere is cheerful, and there is entertainment and dancing every night in season. An obliging staff with high standards of service will take care of you. Aghadoe Heights is an altogether agreeable place, well liked by Americans.

On nearby Aghadoe hill, known in song and legend, are ancient castle ruins about 30 feet high, which contain a stairway within 6-foot-thick walls, the lower section of a round tower, and the remnants of a church dating from the seventh century.

Price category: Expensive. *Proprietor:* Louis O'Hara. *Telephone:* (064) 31766. *Closed:* December 20 through mid-January. *Rooms:* 55 with bath, telephone, and television; ground-floor rooms. *Meals:* Luncheon, snacks, tea, dinner for public; full license. *Facilities:* Lounge, cocktail bar, gift shop, garden. *Activities:* Musical entertainment and dancing in season and tennis at the hotel; lake swimming, indoor pool, tennis, squash, riding, boat rental, sauna, and gym nearby. *Credit cards:* Amex, Diners, Master, Visa. *U.S. agent:* Quality. *How to get there:* The hotel, signposted on Route R562 (the Killorglin road), is 2 1/2 miles from the center of Killarney. [T]

CAHERNANE HOTEL

> 'Tis lovely! 'Tis divine! Except in a good old house geni-
> ally decked for Christmas, I have never seen such a
> profusion of holly in any one spot as may be observed
> over and over again along the roads. The truth about
> Killarney is easily told — it is lovely, beautiful as Truth
> itself.
>
> *Sir Francis Burnand*

The words above, by the editor of London's famous magazine *Punch*, still do very nicely to describe Killarney a century or so later. William Wordsworth called it the most beautiful spot in the British Isles, even more beautiful than his beloved English lakes of Cumbria.

If you want a short trip back in time to the days of Queen Victoria, then the Cahernane is the place to stay. Built in 1877, it was the luxurious vacation home of the Herbert family. The character of the public rooms is still nineteenth century, with furnishings to reflect the period. A unique Victorian staircase leads to pretty bedrooms, nicer than those in the modern wing. Ask for one with windows framing the view of lake, islands, and mountains, the scenery that prompted the plump little English queen to declare, "Killarney is fairyland." The award-winning dining room offers a nice balance between Continental cuisine and Irish specialties on its extensive à la carte menu, as well as a long list of wines.

Cahernane's 200 acres of pasture and woodland encompass the last 2 miles of the river Flesk as it flows into Lough Leane from the mountains. Flocks of wild swans swim lazily on the lake's waters, and you can wind your way among its islands in a boat arranged by the hotel. Just up the road is Killarney National Park, an estate of 11,000 acres that was presented to the Irish nation by Mr. and Mrs. Bowers Bourne of California and their son-in-law, Senator Arthur Vincent. Among its many attractions is Muckross House, the mansion on the estate, with a museum of Kerry folk life. Here a weaver, a blacksmith, and a potter work at their trades. Woodland trails where Irish red deer and Japanese sika deer are commonly seen are bordered by exotic trees and shrubs. You can order a bicycle through the hotel, with which you can cover more of the park than is possible on foot. At Cahernane you can delight in scenery that drew raves from the pens of the world's great writers.

Price category: Expensive. *Manager:* Conor O'Connell. *Telephone:* (064) 31895. *Closed:* December to Easter except December 20–January 6. *Rooms:* 52 with bath and telephone; TV on request. Christmas and New Year's program. *Meals:* Snacks, tea, dinner for public; full license. *Children:* Baby-sitting. *Facilities:* Lounge, TV lounge, conservatory, cocktail bar, gift shop, garden. *Activities:* Tennis, boats, river fishing, par-3 golf, and bicycles at the hotel; lake swimming and fishing, indoor pool, riding, squash, sauna, and gym nearby. *Credit cards:* Amex, Diners, Master, Visa. *U.S. agent:* RS. *How to get there:* The hotel is on Route N71 (Kenmare Road), 1 mile from Killarney. Guests can be met at Shannon or Dublin airport or the Killarney railway station.[T]

CARRIGLEA

> The arbutus thrives . . . the turf is of livelier hue than elsewhere; the hills glow with a richer purple; the varnish of the holly and ivy is more glossy, the berries of a brighter red peep through foliage of a brighter green.
>
> *Thomas Macaulay*

The combination of a splendid view, old-fashioned charm, and prices that have an antique tinge make Carriglea one of the best values in Killarney. It sits on a rise, back across the road from the lake. From it you will see a panoramic vista of a rugged mountain range, a mighty backdrop for the fabled lakes. Across the water Purple Mountain rises; to the left are Torc and Mangerton, on whose summit is the Devil's Punch Bowl; and to the right is Carrantuohill, Ireland's highest peak. Brendan Behan said that there are many famous experiences that disappoint, but two things that did not disappoint him were his first taste of champagne and his first look at the Lakes of Killarney. If you first see the lakes from Carriglea, you will not be disappointed either. Cooking here is based on produce from the home farm, just as in the days when no one expected food to come from any place except the local fields.

Carriglea adjoins Killarney National Park, where you can view the flowering shrubs extolled by Macaulay in the quotation above. He doesn't mention the great trees of rhododendron that arch over the roads to form tunnels of living beauty, especially in May when they are in bloom. Carriglea's own jaunting cars will take you along at a pace that will allow you to absorb all the splendor. At this hospitable guesthouse you will see the best of Killarney.

Price category: Very inexpensive. *Proprietors:* Michael and Marie Beazley. *Telephone:* (064) 31116. *Closed:* November to Easter. *Rooms:* 9, 6 with bath; ground-floor rooms. *Meals:* Dinner for guests; no license. *Children:* Baby-sitting. *Facilities:* Lounge, garden. *Activities:* Jaunting-car rides at the house; lake swimming, indoor pool, tennis, squash, riding, boat rental, sauna, and gym nearby. *How to get there:* Carriglea is on Route N71 (Kenmare Road) 2 miles from Killarney. Guests can be met at the Killarney railway station.   [T]

THE GARDENS

> There was once a Frenchman, I am told, who said that
> Ireland was the jewel of the West, that Kerry was the
> jewel of Ireland, that Killarney was the jewel of
> Kerry. . . .
>
> *H.V. Morton,* 1931

The scenery, not the town, of Killarney is the jewel of Kerry, and Mrs.
O'Reilly will help you arrange to see the famous sights. Tours by bus
or horse-drawn vehicle all start close to The Gardens. You might like
a ride in a jaunting car along the lake shore.

The setting of this professional guest house is unusual, a three-
minute walk from the town center but secluded behind high, shelter-
ing stone walls that once protected the gardens of Lord Kenmare.
Guests enjoy sitting out on a manicured lawn that is bordered by bright
beds of flowers and shaded by ancient apple trees.

The building and its furnishings are modern except for an enorn-
mous antique oak sideboard that adds interest to the breakfast room.
You enter a roomy lounge with picture windows overlooking the
garden. Small, neat bedrooms with unit furniture and good reading
lights open from a covered walkway. Ask to see what is available since
some are larger than others.

Mrs. O'Reilly will arrange a day's pony trekking, fix you up with
a fishing permit, book a bus tour of the ring of Kerry, or recommend
restaurants, pubs, and shops. The Gardens is a good choice for train
travelers; it's a very short walk from the railway station.

Price category: Very inexpensive. *Proprietor:* Mary O'Reilly. *Telephone:* (064) 31147. *Closed:* November to March. *Rooms:* 21, 19 with
bath. *Children:* Baby-listening. *Facilities:* Lounge, TV lounge, garden.
Activities: Lake swimming, indoor pool, squash, riding, boat rental,
sauna and gym nearby. *How to get there:* From town, start out Muckross Road. Take the first left, Countess Road, to The Gardens.

GREAT SOUTHERN HOTEL

> Civil War history has been written in blood on the steps
> of the Great Southern Hotel; in this building too, the
> loyal and royal of Kerry immured themselves when in
> 1867 the Fenians came marching on snow-sodden
> brogues from Cahirciveen with a tattered green rag flut-
> tering over them.
>
> *Bryan MacMahon*

In contrast to its memories of tragic times — the hotel was occupied by
the Free State forces in the bitter civil war in 1922 — this crown jewel
of the Great Southern Hotels also recalls times of great elegance. It
opened its doors in 1853 to those who lived in Victorian high style. It
is surely the most elegant of the old-time Irish hotels. Young ladies in
garden-party hats and white kid gloves, escorted by young men carrying straw boaters and canes, would have looked more appropriate to
the setting than did our teen-agers in dungarees and old sneakers when
we dragged them in for lunch so that we could get our first look at the
famous place.

In the imposing, high-ceilinged entrance lounge our sandwich lunch
from large silver trays was reminiscent of a formal Victorian tea party;
our children were charmed by the gracious, smiling service. Nothing
stuffy here! (But where in Ireland is anything ever stuffy?) The
elaborate, domed dining room was honored with Bord Failte's "Award
of Excellence."

The hotel is set in 40 acres of garden in the center of Killarney. The
train deposits guests at the door, and bus tours find this a favorite stopping place.

Price category: Very expensive. *Manager:* Michael Rosney. *Telephone:* (064) 31262. *Rooms:* 180, and suites, with bath, telephone, and
TV; suitable for wheelchair guests. *Meals:* Luncheon, snacks, tea, dinner for public; full license. Christmas and New Year's programs. *Children:* Baby-sitting and -listening. *Facilities:* Lounges, cocktail bar, gift
shop, beauty salon, barber, valet, laundry, and 24-hour room service.
Activities: Indoor pool, tennis, and sauna, at the hotel; lake swimming,
boat rental, riding, squash, and gym nearby. *Credit cards:* Amex, Diners, Master, Visa. *U.S. agent:* C.I.E. Tours. *How to get there:* Trains
run from Dublin, Cork, and Rosslare; the station is next to the hotel.[T]

LINDEN HOUSE

> As for a man coming from London or Dublin and seeing "the whole Lakes in a day," he is an ass for his pains; we should look at these wonderful things leisurely and thoughtfully, and even then blessed is he who understands them.
>
> *William Makepeace Thackeray,* 1842

If you want to follow the advice of Thackeray and spend not one but several days seeing "these wonderful things leisurely and thoughtfully," you'll find a stay at Linden House a bargain. This guest house—the type that seems like a small hotel rather than a private home—has been well run for many years by Mr. and Mrs. Franz Knoblauch. She is Irish; he is German—and he is his own chef. Thye have been joined by chef-son Peter and his wife. The restaurant has acquired a reputation for good food at very reasonable prices. Visitors have a choice of ordering from the à la carte menu in the dining room, which is open to the public, or of taking advantage of the less expensive set dinner served at 6:30 P.M. to house guests only.

Linden House is pleasantly furnished in a plain, straightforward way. The cheerful dining room has such German touches as wicker lampshades hanging over each table and a wooden ceiling. There are an attractive lounge and a garden with white outdoor furniture. Smallish bedrooms with private bathrooms have unit furniture.

The location on a quiet, tree-lined street just a few blocks from the busy town center allows visitors to walk to the shops or to one of the popular pubs that feature evenings of ballad singing.

Price category: Very inexpensive. *Proprietors:* The Knoblauch family. *Telephone:* (064) 31379. *Closed:* Mid-December to mid-January. *Rooms:* 11 with bath; minimum two nights advance reservation in high season. *Meals:* Dinner for the public; wine license. *Children:* Babysitting. *Facilities:* Lounge, TV room, and garden. *Activities:* Lake swimming, indoor pool, squash, riding, boat rental, sauna, and gym nearby. *How to get there:* Linden House is on New Road on the west side of the town.　　　　　　　　　　　　　　　　　　　　　　　　　　[T]

LOCH LEIN FARM

> If you want to experience to the full the enchantment of Killarney, get out on the lake on a calm evening . . . and watch the changing effects of light and shade on the towering hills and the water and the woods as sunset approaches If you have been lucky, and have got a day of that indefinable astonishing Killarney atmosphere, you will admit that . . . you have never seen anything more lovely.
>
> *Robert Praeger,* 1937

To go out one of Killarney's lakes, you can rent a boat right at Loch Lein Farm. This congenial place is a purposely-built guest house, no longer an operating farm, whose acres stretch right to the shore of Loch Lein, called also the Lower Lake. You can arrange to hire a ghillie and fishing gear.

Here you'll meet the other guests easily, probably introduced to them by your hostess, Kathleen Coffey. She's a jolly woman who talks with her guests and can give advice on what's most important to see and do in the time you have in Killarney. One of her sons is the local doctor.

Kathleen doesn't serve dinner, but a five-minute walk up the lane will take you to a restaurant run by other members of the family. You can buy food there too, with which you can walk to a nearby picnic area.

This is the only guest house right on the shore of the Killarney lakes. All bedrooms are on the ground floor. For a famous view at a bargain price, ask for a room facing the lake.

Price category: Very inexpensive. *Proprietor:* Kathleen Coffey. *Telephone:* (064) 31260. *Closed:* November through February. *Rooms:* 14, 10 with bath. *Children:* Baby-sitting. *Facilities:* Living room, garden. *Activities:* Lake swimming and boat rental at the house. *How to get there:* Signposted on Route R562, the Killorglin road, 3 miles west of Killarney.

Killiney, Dublin

COURT HOTEL

The laughing ripples sing their lay,
The sky is blue and o'er the bay
The breeze is blowing free;
For, O, the morning's fresh and fair,
And bright and bracing is the air,
Down by the summer sea.

J. *Ashby-Sterry*

Little Killiney, just south of Dublin, is different from other towns we've seen in Ireland. High stone walls undulate up and down winding hilly streets along the bay, reminding us of Bonchurch on the Isle of Wight. Large residences surrounded by gardens and behind walls were gentlemen's villas in Victorian days, when the new railroads made it practical to have a seaside villa. The Court Hotel began life as a gentleman's villa, but today its many extensions and air of activity give it more the feeling of a resort hotel. Its facade of pale green stucco trimmed with white is set off by palm trees and beds of garden flowers. Extensive lawns stretch to the shore. A private walkway for hotel guests leads to a sandy beach that follows the crescent of the bay for 2 miles. The hotel is a popular place for wedding receptions.

Memories of former days remain in the spacious, high-ceilinged lounge adorned with elaborate plaster moldings and pleasantly furnished, though not with old things. A miscellany of such nautical antiques as ships' wheels and lanterns add interest. Try to stay in the original house — in a room with a bay window facing the Irish Sea. In the new wing, rooms are smaller but neat, and bathrooms have marble floors and walls. As at most old-time resort hotels, the menu is extensive. We counted a choice of twelve starters, eight soups, and thirteen main courses, followed by eight desserts.

If we had reason to spend time in Dublin in the summer, we might stay at the Court and combine a seashore vacation with city pleasures. The train station is adjacent to the hotel grounds, and service to Dublin, 8 miles away, is frequent. When a guest arrives by train, all he has

to do is telephone for a porter and walk over to the hotel. Swimming, fishing, sailing, and water skiing could be enjoyed between trips into Dublin for daytime sightseeing or evening visits to Dublin's legendary pubs and theater. It would be pleasant to return from the city in late afternoon and sit on the terrace to sip a predinner drink.

Price category: Moderate to expensive. *Proprietor:* Niall Kenny. *Telephone:* (01) 851622. *Rooms:* 36 with bath, telephone, and television; elevator. *Meals:* Luncheon, snacks, tea, dinner for public; full license. *Children:* Baby-sitting; playground. *Facilities:* Lounge, cocktail bar, public bar, garden. *Activities:* Ocean swimming at the hotel; tennis, riding, hunting, waterskiing, and sailing nearby. *Credit cards:* Master, Visa. *U.S. Agent:* Robert Reid. *How to get there:* Guests can be met at the Dublin airport or the Killiney railway station. The hotel is 3 miles from the Wales car ferry. If driving, ask directions in town.   [T]

GLENLEE

I'm happy to be back again,
I greet you big and small,
For there's no place else on earth
Just like the homes of Donegal.

Sean MacBride

It's a fine thing to explore the lonely, magnificent countryside in the west of Donegal and to end the day before a turf fire at hospitable Glenlee, a modern Donegal home.

The one-story bungalow looks inviting behind its well-kept lawn bordered with colorful flower beds. Inside you'll find a traditional warm Irish welcome from the O'Keeney family. Simply and neatly furnished, Glenlee offers views of the mountains from its windows. In the living room, where there are records and tapes, guests are quickly exchanging talk of their day's adventures.

Killybegs is one of Ireland's most important fishing ports. Be sure to go to the piers to watch the fishing fleet return with its catch in the late afternoon. Sea gulls swarm around the pier, screaming and diving, as the fish are being unloaded from trawlers.

To the west, handloom weavers at Kilcar spin wool in colors that reflect the tones and textures of the nearby heather-covered glens, rocky mountains, and wild seas. Further along are the cliffs of Slieve League, said to be the highest in Europe.

Price category: Very inexpensive. *Proprietor:* Ellen O'Keeney. *Telephone:* (073) 31026. *Closed:* October through February. *Rooms:* 5, 3 with bath; ground floor rooms. *Meals:* Supper and dinner for guests; no license. *Facilities:* Living room, TV room, garden. *Activities:* Ocean swimming, boat rental, and deep-sea fishing nearby. *Credit cards:* Amex, Master, Visa. *How to get there:* The house is on the right just over one mile west of Killybegs on the Glencolmcille Road.

KILMESSAN STATION HOUSE

> You are in Meath now, I suppose. If you go to Tara
> . . . look all around you . . . and remember me to ev-
> ery hill and wood and ruin, for my heart is there. . . .
> Say I will come back again surely, and maybe you will
> hear pipes in the grass or a fairy horn and the hounds
> of Finn—I have heard them often from Tara.
>
> *Francis Ledwidge,* 1916

Poet Ledwidge never returned to Tara, which can be see from Kilmessan House. He was killed in World War I. Though nothing but simple
earthworks remains at Tara now, it was the seat of the high kings of
Ireland from the Bronze Age to A.D. 1022 and is still visited by those
interested in Irish history.

Converted from a once-busy railway station that was built in 1840
and closed in 1963, this little place of lodging is different from most
others recommended. It is neither guest house nor hotel but is primar-
ily a restaurant with rooms. The attractive dining room, with plasterwork arches and ceiling, parquet floor, and old fireplace surrounds,
is decorated in soft colors and has won awards for its fine food. Only
fresh local products are used whenever possible.

Nicely furnished bedrooms—not large—have agreeble touches such
as bowls of fresh fruit and vases of flowers. The cocktail bar is the only
living room, but it has comfortable chairs and a fire when it's cool
enough. A pianist plays here three or four evenings a week, year round.
A very pretty garden terrace, with white furniture, is a pleasant place
to have afternoon tea or a drink after sightseeing. The atmosphere is
friendly and appealing, and the hotel is a good choice for anyone wanting to spend a last night near Dublin airport.

Price category: Inexpensive to moderate. *Proprietors:* Christy and
Thelma Slattery. *Telephone:* (046) 25239. *Closed:* Christmas week.
Rooms: 10, 4 with bath, all with telephone and TV; ground-floor
rooms. *Meals:* Luncheon, snacks, tea, dinner for public; full license.
Children: Baby-sitting, playground, playroom. *Facilities:* Cocktail bar,
garden. *Activities:* Tennis at the hotel. *Credit cards:* Amex, Diners,
Visa. *How to get there:* About 3 miles from Trim on the Dublin road,
Route R154, find Kilmessan signposted to the north.   [T]

Knocknarea, Sligo

PRIMROSE GRANGE

The wind has bundled up the clouds high over Knocknarea,
And thrown the thunder on the stones for all that Maeve can
say.

William Butler Yeats

At Primrose Grange, perched on the side of Knocknarea, you will be
in the midst of what the poet Yeats called "The Land of Heart's Desire."

A path leads from the house to the top of the mountain, Yeats's
"cairn-heaped grassy hill," where a Bronze Age mound of stones 35 feet
high and 600 feet in circumference marks the legendary grave of Maeve,
mythological queen of the Irish fairies, called the *sidhe* (shee). From
here you can see Lough Gill with its isle of Innisfree, Rosses Point, and
the town of Sligo — all places named in his poems. "Bare Ben Bulben,"
the mountain under which Yeats asked to be buried in Drumcliff
churchyard, looms to the north.

Primrose Grange was built in 1723 as a school for boarders. At one
time, students whose families could not pay the full fee were called

"kitchen boarders" because they ate in the kitchen on scraps left after the boys in the dining room had finished their meals. Think of that when inclined to wonder if the old days were better.

A log fire makes the living room cheery. Some Victorian furniture is mixed with plain newer things. Bedrooms are not large. Proprietor Maisie Carter holds a diploma in domestic science. Her home has won the Irish Tourist Board's Farmhouse of the Year award and was a regional winner for the Best Breakfast award. Mixed farming is done on 40 acres overlooking Ballisodare Bay. Primrose Grange will suit a budget traveler.

Price category: Very inexpensive. *Proprietors:* Maisie and Ed Carter. *Telephone:* (071) 62005. *Closed:* December through January. *Rooms:* 8, 1 with bath. *Meals:* Dinner for guests; wine license. *Children:* Baby-sitting. *Facilities:* Lounge, sitting room, garden. *Activities:* Ocean swimming, outdoor pool, boat trips, squash, and riding nearby. *How to get there:* West of Sligo town, in Knocknarea near Strandhill, Primrose Grange, signposted on Route N4, is on a minor road by the south side of Knocknarea Mountain.

ASHTON GROVE

> The reception one meets with from the women of a
> family generally determines the tenor of one's whole
> entertainment.
>
> *Thomas De Quincey,* 1821

At Ashton Grove you will be met with warm hospitality by Nancy Fitz-
Gerald, chairwoman of the Irish Farm Holidays Association. She is
a knowledgeable and amusing conversationalist who knows a lot about
Irish literature, arts, crafts people and more. She'll direct you to all sorts
of interesting things in the area.

Entrance to this secluded Georgian house is through a black iron
gate that leads into beautifully maintained grounds. Thriving flower
beds and large holly trees provide a lovely setting for iron garden furniture. Inside, a living room — with a high, elaborately plastered ceiling and a peat fire under a marble mantel — offers big, comfortable
chairs beside antique mahogany tables holding books and magazines.
The bedrooms contain furnishings from the early eighteenth century.
In the dining room, gleaming with old silver and cut crystal, you'll enjoy excellent country-style cooking based on fresh produce from the
farm.

Those who prefer the country to a city can sleep here while they explore Cork city, fewer than 8 miles away. The obligatory Blarney stone
is close by.

Price category: Very inexpensive. *Proprietor:* Nancy FitzGerald.
Telephone: (021) 821537. *Closed:* Mid-October through April. *Rooms:*
4 with shared baths and shower. *Meals:* Light meals for guests; no
license. *Facilities:* Living room, TV room, garden. *Activities:* Riding
nearby. *How to get there:* Ashton Grove is signposted on N8, the main
Cork-Dublin road, 7 1/2 miles from Cork city.

Lahinch, Clare

ABERDEEN ARMS HOTEL

At Lahinch the sea shines like a jewel.

Percy French

Lahinch itself is the attraction here, and the Aberdeen Arms, within a block of the beach but in the center of town, is the first choice for lodging. The dining room offers fresh, well-cooked, wholesome food, specializing in fish from the sea, local farm fare, and homemade brown bread. The bar attracts a lively mix of locals and visitors.

Lahinch is a summer resort where many well-to-do Irish families have vacation homes. Big breakers roll up the smooth sands of a mile-long beach, setting the scene for some of the best surfing in Ireland. For days too cool to brave the waves, there is a large heated pool at the town's Entertainment Centre, which also offers movies, dancing, and a variety of indoor amusements to suit young children and teenagers. Lahinch has two eighteen-hole golf courses, and we know golf enthusiasts from Boston who vacation every year at the Aberdeen Arms to play the championship links.

Five miles north, the Cliffs of Moher rise sheer out of the sea for 700 feet and extend 5 miles along the wild coast. Sea gulls swoop and glide far below over crashing waves. Doolin, a small fishing village just north along the coast, has become internationally famous as a center for Irish folk music. From there you can take a boat to the Aran Islands, dimly seen in the mist off on the horizon. From Lahinch, make a circular tour of the Burren, that strange region thickly populated in prehistoric times, where up to seven hundred stone forts and dolmens still stand. This is the land of which Cromwell's General Ludlow wrote, "It is a country where there is not enough water to drown a man, wood enough to hang one, nor earth enough to bury him." There *is* water aplenty, but most of it flows in underground rivers.

Those who love vacationing at a beach resort may go straight from Shannon Airport to the Aberdeen Arms and take in a great variety of Ireland's countless scenic and historic wonders without ever changing hotels.

Price category: Moderate. *Manager:* Seamus Logue. *Telephone:* (065) 81100. *Closed:* Mid-October to early April. *Rooms:* 50 with bath and telephone. *Meals:* Snacks, tea, dinner; full license. *Children:* Babysitting. *Facilities:* Lounge, TV room, cocktail bar, public bar, snooker room. *Activities:* Ocean swimming, surfing, outdoor pool, tennis, sauna, deep-sea fishing, boat rental, and boat trips nearby. *Credit cards:* Amex, Diners, Master, Visa. *How to get there:* Lahinch is on the west coast of Clare.   [T]

Letterfrack, Galway

ROSLEAGUE MANOR

> The countryside was faintly magical even in the rain. Half tones told of it; and the soft atmosphere made you feel that you were in a region . . . where there was neither time, nor tide, nor any change at all.
> *Oliver St. John Gogarty*

In the beautiful countryside beloved by the Dublin wit Gogarty, there is a late Georgian house, Rosleague Manor; palm trees and rhododendron on well-kept lawns contrast with the rugged beauty of the cloud-wreathed Twelve Bens rising to the east.

A combination of friendliness, outstanding food, and interesting antiques combine to make this one of our favorite hotels. Antique tables and accessories enhance comfortable living rooms where you can curl up and read before turf fires, although in this friendly place you are more likely to chat with other guests. Anne Foyle, who runs Rosleague with her brother Patrick, introduces people to each other. In the attractive bar, you may meet guests from many countries. Greens and flowers are arranged in old washbowls, and walls are hung with oil paintings, watercolors of local scenes, antique china, and old fans. An Imari plate framed in velvet is unique.

Patrick, or Paddy, is usually to be found in the kitchen. He trained on the Continent, and his cooking prompted one guest, who owned a restaurant in Acapulco, to ask him to chef there in the winter. The

Mexican dishes he learned there in two seasons add to the menu's sophistication. We started one dinner with gazpacho; beef in red wine and Wiener schnitzel were our main courses that evening, but superb local salmon, sea trout, and rack of lamb are the most popular choices. As Paddy prefers Ireland to Mexico, he spent some winters building four housekeeping cottages on the grounds of Rosleague. You can rent them by the week all year.

Letterfrack was founded by Quakers in the early nineteenth century. Connemara Handcrafts, Ltd., just a walk down the road from the hotel, has the most attractive assortment of Irish goods we've seen. It also has a tearoom where light fare is served all day, so be sure to make a stop there if you are just passing through.

Price category: Moderate to expensive. *Proprietors:* Anne and Patrick Foyle. *Telephone:* (095) 41101. *Closed:* November to mid-April. *Rooms:* 11 with bath and telephone; 4 suites; self-catering cottages. *Meals:* Luncheon, snacks, tea, dinner; full license. *Facilities:* Drawing room, sitting room, TV room, library, conservatory, cocktail bar, garden. *Activities:* Tennis and sauna at the manor; salmon, trout, and deep-sea fishing, ocean swimming, boat trips, and riding nearby. *Credit cards:* Amex, Master, Visa. *U.S. agent:* Robert Reid Associates. *How to get there:* The hotel is on Route N59, 8 miles north of Clifden.   [T]

CLONEEN HOUSE

> Let me live in a house by the side of the road
> Where the race of men go by.
>
> *Sam Walter Foss*

Near Shannon Airport, on the main road into Limerick, this is a convenient first or last stop in Ireland, especially for anyone who does not want to drive, because city and airport buses stop at the gate. Daily tours and medieval banquets can be arranged, with guests collected and returned to Cloneen House.

The old house, impeccably maintained, has high ceilings, tile floors, and bay windows. Its decoration is plain, with period furniture here and there. Walls are bedecked with old prints and plates. The only public room is a TV lounge — this is more a city guest house than the sort of country inn where guests gather together in the evening for conversation. Guests often sit on the enclosed lawn edged with beds of bright flowers. There is parking behind the house. Jury's and Ryan's hotels are minutes away on foot, and the center of Limerick is but a ten-minute walk.

Price category: Very inexpensive. *Proprietors:* Bridgit and Robert Power. *Telephone:* (061) 54461. *Rooms:* 7, 3 with bath. *Meals:* Dinner for guests; no license. *Facilities:* TV lounge, garden. *Activities:* Outdoor pool, river swimming, tennis, and squash nearby. *Credit Cards:* Master, Visa. *Mailing address:* Cloneen House, Ennis Road, Limerick. *How to get there:* The house is on Route N18, the main Shannon-Limerick road, on the north side of Limerick.

Lismore, Waterford

LISMORE CASTLE

Beautiful Lismore Castle afforded us much pleasure.
Situated . . . high above the Blackwater River, which
is famed for its salmon fishing. Lismore is rich in tradition and historic charm.

Fred Astaire, 1935

Lismore Castle is owned by the Duke of Devonshire. Adele, sister and first dancing partner of Fred Astaire, married the previous duke's younger brother, and they made Lismore Castle their home. Pictures of Fred are in many of the rooms.

The guest list has been star-studded since Walter Raleigh strode through its paneled rooms. Robert Boyle, the father of modern chemistry, was born here in 1626. King James II dined in its great hall in 1690, and King Edward VII and Queen Alexandra slept in some of the beds you can sleep in now.

Lismore Castle is available by the week for from six to twelve guests in one group. This seems an ideal destination for small business conferences or groups of friends — members of bridge clubs or golf foursomes, perhaps, who go off to a resort together once a year. And what more romantic place could be found for a family gathering?

A tennis court and a 9-hole golf course are right on the estate, and several 18-hole courses in the area welcome guests. The castle is famous for its own salmon, sea-trout, and brown trout fishing on the River Blackwater. Race courses are within easy reach; riding and hunting can be arranged. And Lismore is a central location for day trips to the Rock of Cashel, Waterford, Cork, Killarney, and historic Kilkenny.

The castle is fully staffed with maids, cook, and butler. Mr. Paul Burton, the resident estate manager, lives in a separate wing of the castle and will ensure that everything goes smoothly. Included in the fee are all meals and even personal laundry. You will live as the Duke does when he is in residence.

You may invite friends and relatives to the castle for meals, at an extra charge. If you'd like to meet local citizens, you can arrange with Mr. Burton to invite some to tea, dinner, or a cocktail party. The 6th Duke (1790-1858) liked to dispense hospitality to the neighbors, and for one ball he gave for the "merchants, shopkeepers and respectable inhabitants" of Lismore, he provided the modern-sounding Rock Bell and Steel Band.

Sir Joseph Paxton, who designed the Crystal Palace in London, was responsible for the rehabilitation of the castle and gardens in the mid-nineteenth century. The designing of interiors and furniture at that time was the work of Augustus Pugin, who collaborated in rebuilding the Houses of Parliament. In the garden, some of it enclosed by walls built in 1627, is a Yew Walk and collections of camellias, magnolias, and other shrubs and flowers. Lismore Castle has been beautifully kept up — no faded glory here.

The Marquess of Hartington, who married Kathleen Kennedy, sister of President John F. Kennedy, would have inherited Lismore Castle had he not been killed in action in World War II. A visit to Lismore Castle will be an unforgettable pilgrimage into the past.

Price category: Very expensive. *Manager:* Paul Burton. *Telephone:* (058) 54424. *Rooms:* 10 bedrooms, 7 bathrooms. *Meals:* All meals for guests. *Facilities:* Drawing room, sitting room, billiards room, garden, laundry service. *Activities:* Golf, tennis, and salmon and trout fishing at the castle; riding and hunting nearby. *How to get there:* The castle is in the center of Lismore.

LONGUEVILLE HOUSE

> Beauing, belling, dancing, drinking,
> Breaking windows, damning, sinking,
> Ever raking, never thinking,
> Live the rakes of Mallow.
>
> *Anonymous*

Mallow was once known as the "Irish Bath," attracting thousands of visitors to its spa. The roistering of wealthy young men earned the place a reputation for wild behavior, hard to imagine in the serene atmosphere of Longueville House. Its Presidents' Restaurant, with paintings of Ireland's presidents, is one of the most prestigious in Ireland.

Jane and Michael O'Callaghan developed Longueville House into its present prominence. Much of the food comes from their 500-acre farm and its river, the famous Blackwater: meat, fish, vegetables, and fruit. Sausage, black and white puddings (an Irish specialty), breads, flaky pastry, and jams are homemade, but the menu is sophisticated. Son William, trained in France, is in charge of the kitchen. His cooking and imaginative presentation get high praise in all food guides. Michael selects the wines for an extensive list.

The house was built about 1720 and extensively added to and renovated, in the Georgian manner, in 1795. A Victorian conservatory of glass over curved iron was added in 1866. Lofty ceilings are ornamented with delicately molded plaster-work by Italian artists; a stairway rises three stories. There is something beautiful to look at wherever one turns: rare inlaid mahogany doors with heavy brass hardware, a white marble Adam mantel, Irish silver displayed behind glass doors in the library, fine antique furniture. From our bedroom, looking out over trees planted in the formation of the French and English lines at the Battle of Waterloo, we could see the ruins of Dromineen Castle, ancient home of O'Callaghan ancestors.

Longueville has come full circle. Cromwell took the land from the O'Callaghans, who had owned it back to times before recorded history, and gave it to one of his followers. It came back to the O'Callaghans

when Michael's father bought it in 1934.

Price category: Moderate to expensive. *Proprietors:* The O'Callaghan family. *Telephone:* (022) 47156. *Closed:* Christmas through February. *Rooms:* 16 with bath, telephone, and TV. *Meals:* Dinner for public by reservation; full license. *Children:* Not suitable for those under ten. *Facilities:* Drawing room, library, cocktail bar, garden. *Activities:* Game room at the house; riding, squash, tennis, and indoor pool nearby. *U.S. agents:* Selective Hotels and Robert Reid Associates. *How to get there:* The house is on Route N72, 3 miles west of Mallow.[T]

Maynooth, Kildare

MOYGLARE MANOR HOTEL

To me, not the least delight of travel is the ever-growing
picture-gallery of beauty spots that I gather and treasure in my mind.

James Hissey, 1910

Moyglare Manor is a beauty spot — a Georgian house in parkland surroundings which evokes a lavish era in Irish country-house living. It
was the manor house of a stud farm until recently, when it was turned
into a hotel by one of Ireland's best-known family of hoteliers.

Furnished with an extravagant collection of antiques in mint condition, the house has an exuberant air. Vivacious colors and fires glowing under formal Adam mantels add a feeling of warmth. Throw pillows
in velvet, silk, and needlepoint add comfort to luxurious upholstered
furniture.

In spacious bedrooms, floral fabrics drape four-poster and tester beds. Concessions to twentieth-century living include splendid bathrooms and good central heat. Fresh vegetables and fruit from the manor's own garden and orchard add to the quality of the extensive menu that entices successful Dubliners to drive the eighteen miles for dinner. Several nights a week, there is music in the cocktail bar that encourages many a lively evening of song.

This hotel is popular with the racing crowd. The many stud farms in the surrounding area have been the breeding ground for some of the world's best horses. It is close to Castletown House, a magnificent example of an old Irish mansion, built in 1722 and now open to the public.

Price category: Very expensive. *Manager:* Shay Curran. *Telephone:* (01) 286351. *Closed:* Good Friday and 3 days at Christmas. *Rooms:* 17 with bath; off-season rates. *Meals:* Luncheon and dinner for public; full license. *Children:* Not suitable for children under 12. *Facilities:* Lounge, cocktail lounge, garden. *Activities:* Riding and hunting nearby. *Credit cards:* Amex, Diners, Visa. *U.S. agent:* Robert Reid Associates. *How to get there:* From Dublin, take Route N4 to the west, which goes through the Main Street of Maynooth. After passing Maynooth University, go straight ahead instead of turning with Route N4. The hotel will be signposted.   [T]

BALLYRYAN HOUSE

> You may sail the "Shannon Willow"
> To the sunny shores of Clare,
> Cool in the Glens of Wicklow,
> Or the forests of Kildare.
> But you'll not find the best of Ireland
> Until you rest in the Ryans' care.
>
> *Anonymous*

The verse above, written in the guest book at Ballyryan House, indicates the sort of hospitality you'll find at the home of Pat and Joan Ryan, an eighteenth-century Old-World farmhouse in Ireland's rich, picturesque farmland called "the Golden Vale." Joan takes pride in the personal attention given to each guest and in the food, which is prepared with the freshest of farm produce.

Guests dine together at one long table, then enjoy coffee in a homey living room that has comfortable velvet-upholstered chairs. In good weather, move out to the spacious lawn. If you have children with you, they'll be treated to pony rides here. Beef cattle graze in the surrounding fields.

Nearby are Cahir Castle and Holy Cross Abbey. The castle is now an architectural interpretative center. Holy Cross Abbey was founded in 1168 and, after standing roofless for over 200 years, restored in 1975 as part of the celebration of European Architectural Heritage Year. It is in use as a parish church.

Price category: Very inexpensive. *Proprietors:* Joan and Pat Ryan. *Telephone:* (062) 57790. *Closed:* November to March. *Rooms:* 5 sharing baths. *Meals:* Breakfast and dinner for guests; no license. *Children:* Baby-sitting and pony rides. *Facilities:* Living room and garden. *Activities:* Indoor pool and tennis nearby. *How to get there:* The house is on Route N24, 4 miles north of Tipperary. [T]

Mountrath, Laois

ROUNDWOOD HOUSE

An old house like this—lived in and kept up as it was
in our great forefathers' times of glorious memory . . .
is a priceless treasure.   *James Hissey,* 1885

Roundwood House offers guests an opportunity to step back to another time. The house was left to the Irish Georgian Society by a man who restored it and furnished it with antiques. Today it is owned by the friendly Kennans. Frank has a gift for storytelling.

In a large combination drawing room-library, we found it delightful to sit before a fire, browsing through books we had selected from shelves that line the room, while sipping a glass of wine. Bedrooms are spacious, and bathrooms are modern. The atmosphere is informal and relaxed, and you'll meet the Kennan children.

In season, arrangements can be made for you to join the Laois Hunt which meets twice weekly. It's a colorful spectacle to see if you don't ride. In an area where most hotels are commerical, Roundwood is a pleasant alternative.

Price category: Inexpensive. *Proprietors:* Rosemarie and Frank Kennan. *Telephone:* (0502) 32120. *Rooms:* 7 with bath. *Meals:* Dinner for the public by reservation; wine license. *Children:* Baby-sitting, playground, playroom. *Facilities:* Drawing room-library, sitting room, garden. *Activities:* Trout, salmon, and coarse fishing, tennis, riding, and hunting nearby. *How to get there:* From Mountrath, start towards Ballyfin, turn left into the road marked Kinnity and drive 3 miles.

REDCASTLE HOTEL

> Donegal comes first. I choose it because there is no-
> where else where the beauties of hill and dale, lake and
> rock, sea and bog, pasture and tillage, are so intimate-
> ly and closely interwoven.
>
> *Robert Praeger,* 1937.

The Redcastle Hotel is a professional hotel that is warm and personal. Large open fireplaces give all lounges a welcoming air. Some public rooms have oak beams, others are decorated with beautiful floral fabrics. Antique pieces and many oil paintings are used for accent. A sun lounge that affords grand views over Lough Foyle leads to a terrace above the water. We liked having a snack or a drink there while watching the activity on the beach below. Exceptionally comfortable bedrooms, with dressing areas, have good modern bathrooms with heated towel bars. A 9-hole golf course, with another nine holes to be added, starts outside the door (clubs can be rented). Extensive gardens are meticulously cared for. Finding this very attractive hotel away up near the northeast tip of the Irish Republic, in what we thought might be an isolated area, was a pleasant surprise.

Price category: Moderate to expensive. *Manager:* Betty McIntyre. *Telephone:* (077) 82073. *Rooms:* 35 with bath, telephone, and TV; 2-day reduction midweek. *Meals:* Lunch, snacks, tea, and dinner for public; full license. *Children:* Baby-listening. *Facilities:* Lounge, sun lounge, cocktail lounge, garden. *Activities:* Ocean-swimming, indoor pool, free golf, tennis, Jacuzzi, sauna at the hotel; riding nearby. *Credit cards:* Amex, Diners, Master, Visa. *How to get there:* The hotel is on Route T75 south of Moville. [T]

LORUM OLD RECOTRY

> It is clear that for a stranger the Irish ways are the
> pleasantest for here he is at once made happy and at
> home.
>> *William Makepeace Thackeray,* 1842

You'll quickly feel at home in this attractive old house, and you'll soon be on a first-name basis with other guests who gather in the drawing room before dinner, around the log fire glowing in a white marble fireplace. Books abound throughout the house, including the bedrooms, some of which have fireplaces with black marble mantels.

The house is furnished almost entirely with Irish antiques of mahogany. There is an elegant Sheraton sideboard in the dining room, where guests sit down to dinner at one long oval Victorian table, gleaming with years of loving care and set with table mats. The cooking is outstanding — everything is homemade and nicely presented.

Lorum Old Rectory won a regional award for Farmhouse of the Year for southeastern Ireland. On the farm are goats, sheep, Angora rabbits, horses, cattle and a donkey.

Muine Bheag (for pronunciation, you're on your own!) is only 15 miles from the medieval city of Kilkenny, where there is much to see.

Price category: Very inexpensive. *Proprietor:* Mrs. Bobbie Smith. *Telephone:* (0503) 75282. *Rooms:* 5 sharing baths. *Meals:* Dinner for guests; wine license. *Children:* Baby-sitting; play yard. *Facilities:* Living room, garden. *Activities:* River swimming, trout and salmon fishing, outdoor pool, tennis, and riding nearby. *How to get there:* The house is on Route R705, 4 miles south of Muine Bheag.

KILLAGHY CASTLE HOUSE

Castle of ancient days! in time long gone
Thy lofty halls in royal splendor shone!
Thou stood'st a monument of strength sublime,
A giant laughing at the threats of time!

James Bird

This Norman castle, whose history can be traced to 1206, could have come from an Irish saga. Haunted by centuries of conquest and rebellion, its empty shell towers over an adjoining eighteenth-century farm-manor guest house. From an upper floor of the farmhouse, Mrs. Sherwood opened a door to let us look into what was once a feudal fortified castle. Brave and agile young historians sometimes climb onto stone ledges, which supported long-gone floors, and clamber up narrow stone stairs that hug the well-preserved walls. The wind soughs through, and birds dart in and out of narrow slits from which deadly arrows once found their mark. We shivered and turned to the warm comfort of today's guest house.

Bedrooms are large, and the house is furnished with old oak, brass beds, and other reminders of past generations. The comfortable drawing room invites evenings of conversation around a log fire, and high ceilings display elaborate plasterwork. In the dining room, where you may sit with other guests or at separate tables, you can have dinner or high tea (supper) if you let Mrs. Sherwood know in time which you want. Breads and desserts are home-baked.

A walled garden is a protected place to sit outside on sunny days. There are views of Slievenaman, one of Ireland's "enchanted mountains" where fairies, or *sidhe* (shee), are said to live near the summit and ride down the moonbeams into the valleys.

Price category: Very inexpensive. *Proprietor:* Mrs. Ruby Sherwood. *Telephone:* (052) 53112. *Closed:* Mid-October through March. *Rooms:* 4 with 2 shared baths. 3-day reduction. *Meals:* Dinner for guests; no license. *Children:* Baby-sitting. *Facilities:* Drawing room, garden. *How to get there:* The castle is near Mullinahone on the Ballingarry road.

GAINSTOWN HOUSE

> Tired with the town and all its noisy say,
> With eager haste I made the northern way,
> Leave pomp and vanity, fatigue and care,
> For sweet tranquility with rural fare.
>
> *Thomas Maude,* 1771

Gainstown House is north of Dublin and a place "for sweet tranquility with rural fare." This period house seems more like a fine suburban home than a farm house, but the Reillys raise beef cattle and tillage. In luxuriously carpeted rooms, furniture is a fine mix of old and new; and plants abound. The food is rural fare at its best. A terrace surrounded by flower gardens is a peaceful place to sit and read or enjoy a cup of tea. Guests meet in a spacious living room.

A nephew and his wife said this was one of their favorite stops during a month's visit to Ireland, staying entirely in private-home guest houses. In a prosperous area close to Dublin and its airport, Gainstown House is a good first or last night's lodging.

Price category: Very inexpensive. *Proprietor:* Mrs. Mary Reilly. *Telephone:* (046) 21448. *Closed:* November through March. *Rooms:* 4, 1 with bath. *Meals:* Dinner for guests; no license. *Children:* Baby-sitting, play-yard. *Facilities:* Living room, garden. *Activities:* Indoor pool and tennis nearby. *How to get there:* The house is 1 mile off the Navan-Trim road, 2 miles from Navan on Route N3.

LIMETREE LODGE

> When my feet first trod Irish soil I felt that I had come to a magic country and now, as I said goodbye, I knew it truly as an enchanted island.
>
> *H. V. Morton,* 1931

When you are ready to say goodbye to Ireland, you might spend your last night at Limetree Lodge if it's on your way to Shannon airport.

This attractively furnished home of the Geary family is about 200 years old. It stays open all winter, so you'll be happy to find electric blankets in bedrooms that are decorated with pretty florals. Bathrooms have bidets and those lovely heated bars to warm the bath towels that we almost never see at home.

Velvet draperies frame a bay window in a large living room, where big comfortable chairs are drawn up before a fire. We ate some of the best scones in Ireland here when we arrived at tea time. Baked by Peggy Geary herself, they are served with her homemade jam. Lucky guests get them again when Peggy brings tea to the living room before bedtime, a delightful custom practiced by the nicest private-home lodgings.

In good weather you might have your afternoon tea or second cup of breakfast coffee while sitting in the sun on garden furniture. For hominess and hospitality, Limetree Lodge gets good marks.

Price category: Very inexpensive. *Proprietor:* Mrs. Peggy Geary. *Telephone:* (069) 62366. *Closed:* Christmas. *Rooms:* 4, 2 with bath. *Meals:* Dinner for guests; no license. *Children:* Baby-sitting. *Facilities:* Living room, conservatory, garden. *How to get there:* The house is on Route N21 one mile south of Newcastle West.

DROMOLAND CASTLE HOTEL

> I dislike to feel at home when I'm abroad.
> *George Bernard Shaw*

You'll never feel at home at Dromoland Castle, not unless home is the quintessence of opulence. An article in *Esquire* magazine called this one of the eight most luxurious resorts in the world. From 1570 until 1963, when it was transformed into a sumptuous hotel, it was the seat of the O'Brien clan. They descended in an unbroken line from the high king, Brian Boru, victor over the Danes at Clontarf in 1014.

O'Brien ancestral portraits lining the wide corridors are reminders of the castle's historic past, but it is difficult today to connect these handsomely furnished and decorated rooms with the scenes of combat, intrigue, and revelry they once beheld. In 1803, William Smith O'Brien, leader of the Young Ireland movement, was born here. He was one of the best known of the thousands of patriots who fought in the recurring struggles to win Ireland's freedom.

President Richard M. Nixon held a reception at Dromoland Castle in 1970. Only 8 miles from Shannon Airport, it is a favorite first stop for many Americans. Golfing on its eighteen-hole course and trolling for trout in its lake are just some of the activities at this complete resort. If you plan to drive through Ireland's mountains and valleys, you can taxi from the airport to Dromoland Castle and later have your hired car delivered to the door. Now owned by an American company, and catering to many tour groups, Dromoland Castle is the answer for those who crave the romance of medieval living but want a professional hotel atmosphere.

Price category: Very expensive. *Manager:* Mark Nolan. *Telephone:* (061) 71144. *Rooms:* 75 with bath, TV, and telephone; 6 suites; suitable for wheelchair guests. Christmas and New Year's programs. *Meals:* Luncheon, snacks, tea, dinner for public; full license. *Children:* Babysitting; playground. *Facilities:* Drawing room, lounge, TV lounge, cocktail bar, billiard room, gift shop, garden. *Activities:* Golf, tennis, row-

boats, and fishing at the hotel; riding, hunting, and deep-sea fishing nearby. *Credit cards:* Amex, Carte Blanche, Diners, Master, Visa. *U.S. agent:* Ashford Castle, Inc. *How to get there:* From Shannon airport take Route N18 north about 3 miles; guests can be met at Shannon airport or the Limerick or Ennis railway station.　　　　　　　[T]

NEWPORT HOUSE

No life, my honest scholar, no life so happy and so
pleasant as the life of a well governed angler.
Izaak Walton, 1653

This time-mellowed building covered with ivy was home to the
O'Donels, earls of Tyrconnell, for two hundred years; before that the
demesne was a stronghold of Grainne Uí Mhaille (Grace O'Malley),
the legendary Sea Queen of the West. Most of the present building dates
from about 1720. For those interested in architecture, the house is worth
visiting just to see the unique staircase in the center of the building.
A glass-domed roof floods the stairwell with light right to the large
ground-floor hall. Elaborate plaster-work cove moldings edge the dome
and define the second-floor ceiling level. The broad stairway divides
into two at a landing and joins again to sweep to the top floor. Valuable
tables with rope-turned legs, unique corner chairs, a breakfront filled
with old books, large silver serving pieces, and oil paintings in heavy
gilt frames are some the antiques that furnish the stair hall. Beautiful
fabrics and rugs decorate the public rooms. We prefer bedrooms in the
main house to those in other buildings on the grounds.

Newport House is undoubtedly one of the most famous fishing
hotels in Ireland. A fisheries director makes arrangements to give each
fisherman an ideal holiday. Write for the fishing brochure and reserve
a boat and ghillie.

Price category: Moderate. *Proprietors:* Kieran and Thelma Thomp-
son. *Telephone:* (098) 41222. *Closed:* October to mid-March. *Rooms:*
20 with bath; TV available. *Meals:* Snacks, tea, dinner for public; full
license. *Facilities for children:* Baby-sitting. *Facilities:* Drawing room,
lounge, billiard room, public bar, game room, garden, and laundry.

NEWPORT HOUSE · THE GALLERY

Activities: Salmon and sea-trout fishing and boat trips at the house; ocean swimming, riding, and tennis nearby. *Credit cards:* Amex, Diners, Master, Visa. *U.S. agent:* Robert Reid. *How to get there:* The house is on Route N59 in Newport. Guests can be met at the Westport railway station.   [T]

Oughterard, Galway

CURRAREVAGH HOUSE

> A more beautiful village can scarcely be seen than this.
> It stands upon Lough Corrib, the banks of which are
> here . . . picturesque and romantic: and a pretty river,
> the Feogh, comes rushing over rocks and by woods
> until it passes the town and meets the lake.
> *William Makepeace Thackeray*, 1842

Among the country-house hotels of Ireland, Currarevagh is a master-piece. To find it in the village that enchanted Thackeray, you'll go down a long driveway bordered with rhododendron in profusion to an isolated ivy-covered Victorian manor. The estate contains 140 wooded acres ''upon Lough Corrib, the banks of which are here . . . picturesque and romantic,'' and Harry Hodgson holds sporting rights to 5,000 acres more of moorland stocked with grouse, woodcock, and snipe.

The interior of the house is appropriate to the inviting quality of the approach. The mood is country-gentleman. Currarevagh (pronounced Curra re' va) has been home to five generations of the Hodgson family. It owes much of its character to nothing being abandoned that was once good; everything is the best of its own day. A gong announces dinner. In the dining room each table and set of chairs are from a different period. While you'll have no choice, the four courses will be some of the best food you'll enjoy on your trip. The main course is usually a roast garnished with vegetables from nearby farms. Seconds are offered. Dessert might be a soufflé with heavy cream that is also right from the farm. The cooking, which rates superlatives in food guides, is served only to guests. Many regular guests return year after year, especially in May and June when the fishing is best.

Price category: Moderate. *Proprietors:* Harry and June Hodgson. *Telephone:* (091) 82313. *Closed:* Late October to late March. *Rooms:* 16 with bath. *Meals:* Snacks and dinner for guests; full license. *Facilities:* Drawing room, sitting room, TV room, garden. *Activities:* Tennis, fishing, lake swimming, boat rides, and boat rental at the house. *U.S. agent:* Robert Reid Associates. *How to get there:* The house is signposted in Oughterard, which is on Route N59 north of Galway.

Oughterard, Galway

LAKELAND

> The traveler . . . gets a view of the wide sheet of Lough Corrib shining in the sun, as we saw it, with its low dark banks stretching round it.
> *William Makepeace Thackeray,* 1842

Hidden away on the banks of Lough Corrib, Lakeland is a family home that was built to be a guest house as well, and a good job was done, too. You'll receive the traditional, warm Irish welcome from Mary and Lal Faherty. Guests exchange their day's experiences around a turf fire in the pleasantly furnished living room, which has window walls that lead out to a lawn and garden. The dining room, where generous portions of home-cooked food are served, commands a view of the lake, as do some of the bedrooms.

This is a fisherman's paradise. Lal will fix you up with gear and either a rowboat or an outboard to catch salmon, trout, or perch. Mary will pack you a lunch, so you can picnic on one of the numerous islands on this great lake, where some ancient ruins still stand. You can swim from a sandy beach right on the property. If boating is not your interest, this is a fine place from which to explore lonely, mysterious Connemara. And a stroll along the lake shore at sunset will be a happy

memory to carry home.

Price category: Very inexpensive. *Proprietors:* Ma
herty. *Telephone:* (091) 82121. *Closed:* Mid-October t
Rooms: 10, 8 with bath. Suitable for wheelchair guest
ner for guests; wine license. *Children:* Baby-sitting. *Fa*
room, TV lounge, garden. *Activities:* Lake swimming, b
rides, fishing at the house; riding and tennis nearby. *H*
The house is signposted on Route N59 about two miles south of Oughterard and 16 miles north of Galway. Guests can be met at the bus stop
in Oughterard. [T]

Oughterard, Galway

OUGHTERARD HOUSE HOTEL

> Do ye know Oughterard with the stream running through it;
> The bridge that falls down on one side like a hill;
> The trees and the pleasant, respectable houses;
> The white waterfall and the old ruined mill.
>
> *Oliver St. John Gogarty*

Oughterard House will call "Come in" to you. Set amid gardens behind a low fence, its Georgian front is mantled in ivy; the stream that
Gogarty mentions above tumbles along on the far side of the road.

Frequently called Sweeney's Oughterard House, or just Sweeney's,
it is an attractive hotel to walk into. Lounges with period furnishings
have old-fashioned charm. Because of the popularity of the hotel's dining room, an extension was added that blends nicely with the old house.
Its windows look out on a secluded garden, a pleasant setting for the
good meals served. A large bar where guests gather during the evening
is furnished in a modern style and offers an extensive bar-food menu.
Try to get one of the old bedrooms in the main house; those in a modern
extension are more plainly decorated.

Oughterard is a famous angling center. Close by is Ross Castle,
birthplace of Violet Martin, who became the Martin Ross of the
late-nineteenth-century Somerville and Ross literary partnership.

Price category: Moderate to expensive. *Proprietors:* Patric and Maire Higgins. *Telephone:* (091) 82207. *Closed:* December 24–28. *Rooms:* 20 with bath, telephone, and tea-making. suitable for wheelchair guests. *Meals:* Luncheon, snacks, tea, dinner for public; full license. *Children:* Baby-sitting; children's meals. *Facilities:* Sitting room, public bar, garden, laundry service. *Activities:* Tennis, lake swimming, riding, and boat rental nearby. *Credit cards:* Amex, Diners, Master, Visa. *U.S. agent:* RS. *How to get there:* The hotel is on Route N59 in Oughterard, which is between Galway and Clifden. Guests can be met at Shannon airport or the Galway railway station. A bus from Galway will drop you at the door.   [T]

ROSS LAKE HOUSE HOTEL

> In Connemara there are no destinations—only pauses.
> Pause as you feel inclined. You never get anywhere
> by going on. There is nowhere to get to!
>
> *Sean O'Faolain*

You'll enjoy a pause at Ross Lake House, which is in that part of County Galway called "the gateway to Connemara." A long drive through five acres of landscaped gardens and past a tennis court will bring you to a Georgian mansion where you'll be welcomed by Henry and Elaine Reid.

Previous owners had "modernized" this lovely old house with many plastic and plywood touches. We were happy to see what the Reids have accomplished in the restored rooms that have been done over with pretty wallpapers and furnished in an old style. Excellent new bathrooms have been installed—one place where we all like the modern touch—and many guests appreciate the modern sauna.

Ross Lake House is a congenial place where it's easy to meet the other guests. The rates are reasonable for a country-house hotel.

Price category: Moderate. *Proprietors:* Henry and Elaine Reid. *Telephone:* (091) 80109. *Rooms:* 12 with bath and telephone. Christmas program. *Meals:* Dinner for the public; full license. *Children:* Babysitting. *Facilities:* Sitting room, TV room, sun room, cocktail bar. *Activities:* Tennis and sauna at the house; riding and boat rental nearby. *Credit cards:* Amex, Diners, Master, Visa. *How to get there:* The hotel is signposted about three miles south of Oughterard on Route N59.[T]

Parknasilla, Kerry

GREAT SOUTHERN HOTEL

> I cannot write seriously about Parknasilla; I cannot
> believe Parknasilla. I awaken each morning and pull
> up the blind to see if the Drury Lane transformation
> scene of yesterday has vanished — but there it all is —
> the fantastic labyrinth of landlocked sea and gardens
> . . . with their winding waterways and interplay of rock
> and foliage, their little bridges flung across fairy chan-
> nels to Liliput islands, are here a thousand times mag-
> nified, in the hotel grounds of Parknasilla.
>
> *Twells Brex*

The same scene that drew such enthusiasm from Brex, a nineteenth-century English journalist, enchants guests today at this Victorian dowager of a hotel on the celebrated Ring of Kerry. The large luxury
establishment began life as the palace of the bishops of Limerick and
was later the home of the father of poet Alfred Graves.

Guests can enjoy themselves for weeks without ever leaving its 300
acres. Stables provide horses for trotting along palm-fringed bridle
paths or trekking with an instructor into the surrounding hills. Tennis
courts and a golf course overlook the islet-studded bay. Warmed by
the Gulf Stream, Parknasilla enjoys some of the mildest climate in
Ireland, and its indented shoreline provides secluded coves for swimming and sunning. You can fish from shore or leave the private jetty
in a boat from the hotel's little fleet — a cabin cruiser, speedboats, sailboats, and rowboats. Inside the gabled graystone mansion are a glass-
walled heated pool, sauna, sun lounge, billiards, and table tennis, as
well as music and dancing in season. A hall porter will arrange for anything you want to do. To keep up the illusion that you are living in the
gracious past, ask for an old-style bedroom, not one in the modern
wing.

A hostelry such as this has had its share of visiting celebrities. The
memory of George Bernard Shaw, who wrote part of *Saint Joan* here
in 1924, is recalled at the Pygmalion Restaurant and the Doolittle Bar.
Charles de Gaulle came after he retired as president of France. If you

cannot spend the night, be sure to stop by to marvel at the palms and subtropical flora, lunch on the terrace and watch water-skiers far below, or take afternoon tea and scones before a fire.

Price category: Very expensive. *Manager:* Jim Feeney. *Telephone:* (064) 45122. *Closed:* Mid-November to Easter. *Rooms:* 59, and suites, with bath, telephone, and TV; ground-floor rooms. *Meals:* Luncheon, snacks, tea, dinner for public; full license. *Children:* Baby-sitting and -listening. *Facilities:* Drawing room, lounge, cocktail bar, sun parlor, billiard room, garden, laundry, valet, and 24-hour room service. *Activities:* Golf, indoor pool, ocean swimming, tennis, riding, boat rides, boat rental, sailing lessons, waterskiing, shore fishing, sauna, game room, and dancing at the hotel; deep-sea, lake, and river fishing nearby. *Credit cards:* Amex, Diners, Master, Visa. *U.S. agent:* C.I.E. Tours. *How to get there:* The hotel is on the Ring of Kerry (Route N70), 17 miles west of Kenmare. Guests can be met at Shannon or Cork airport or the Killarney railway station.   [T]

Prosperous, Kildare

CURRYHILLS HOUSE HOTEL

Stranger, what e'er thy land or creed or race,
Here rest awhile, there's virtue in the place.
Anonymous

Curryhills House, built in 1780, was a Georgian farm guest house. The friendly Traverses have now turned it into a hotel. A wing of nicely decorated small bedrooms with good modern bathrooms has been added, as has a spacious bar lounge. The dining room — which had already earned a reputation for serving good dinners to the public, as well as to house guests — has been enlarged. Turkey raised on the farm and fresh fish from nearby rivers are often on the menu, as well as steak and venison.

Wheat and barley are the main crops of the farm, which Bill Travers still operates. He also raises and runs a race horse or two. The "sport of kings" is followed by many in Ireland, and the Curragh, where the Irish Sweepstakes is run, is nearby. The dining room and bar are frequently filled with convivial race fans who have just enjoyed a day at the track. It's an easy drive to the National Stud and Horse Museum, just outside Kildare town. The famous Japanese Gardens are there too.

If you have been touring through Ireland, you may want to spend a night at this inexpensive hotel before visiting Dublin. Rather than drive into Dublin in late-afternoon traffic, we find it more pleasant to stay a short distance outside the city and then drive in after the morning commuters' rush is over.

Price category: Moderate. *Proprietors:* Bill and Bridie Travers. *Telephone:* (045) 68150 or 68336. *Closed:* December 23–31. *Rooms:* 10 with bath, telephone, and tea-making; suitable for wheelchair guests. *Meals:* Snacks and tea for guests; dinner for the public; full license. *Children:* Baby-sitting. *Facilities:* Living room, sitting room, cocktail lounge, garden. *Activities:* Indoor pool, tennis, and riding nearby; traditional Irish music Friday evenings; sing-a-longs Saturday and Sunday evenings. *Credit cards:* Amex, Master, Visa. *U.S. agent:* RS. *How to get there:* The hotel is on Route R403. [T]

THE MANSE

> I'm happy to be back again
> I greet you big and small
> For there's repose for weary wanderers
> In the Homes of Donegal.
>
> *Sean MacBride*

There is repose for weary wanderers in the delightful home of Mrs. Scott, widow of a minister and a great conversationalist. She came to The Manse as a bride of twenty. Little in it has changed since.

We'd welcome a rainy day to spend in the library, where velveteen draperies went up in 1871. Beside a leather chair, in front of the fragrant fire, we'd stack some of the wonderful old books from the shelves. Then we'd read all day while drinking cups of tea. Mrs. Scott added the antique Persian rug to this room. When she asked her son how he liked it, he replied, "It's like everything else in your home, Mother. Pleasantly shabby."

Shabby is *not* a word we'd apply to The Manse — mellow, perhaps, would be better. This home has grown old gracefully, lived in and loved for a long time. The original part of the house was built in 1690, but the feeling today is of a comfortable Victorian. The living room has hand-blown glass in the curved bay window and chairs and a sofa covered with flowered cretonne. Mahogany antiques furnish the dining room. There are toys about that belonged to Mrs. Scott's great-grandmother. In one bathroom is an antique shower installed in 1900; water sprays from its sides as well as from overhead.

Mrs. Scott was invited to speak at the tercentennial celebration, in Maryland in 1983, of the Presbyterian Church in America, which was established there by Reverend Francis McKemie, who was ordained in the church next to The Manse. He sailed to Chesapeake Bay in 1682.

Price category: Very inexpensive. *Proprietor:* Mrs. Florence Scott. *Telephone:* (074) 51047. *Closed:* Mid-September to Easter, except by reservation. *Rooms:* 4 sharing baths. *Facilities:* Living room, library, garden. *Smoking:* Not permitted in bedrooms. *Activities:* Ocean swimming, tennis, trout fishing, boat rental, and riding nearby. *How to get there:* Ramelton (sometimes spelled Rathmelton) is on Route R245, 6 1/2 miles north of Letterkenny. Ask in town for directions to The Manse, next to the Presbyterian Church.

Rathmullan, Donegal

FORT ROYAL

> There must be some magic connected with the sea. It
> filled me with such delight that . . . it would gladden
> your heart.
>
> *Maurice O'Sullivan*, 1933

A pleasant, quiet country house in historic Rathmullan, Fort Royal is
set in 18 acres of lawn and woodland bordering a sheltered sea lough
in rugged northwestern Donegal. The decorating and the modern furnishings do not match the exterior of the house or its setting, but everything is bright, clean, and comfortable. Flowers in casual arrangement
ornament the rooms, where logs and peat burning in the fireplaces add
to the atmosphere. Fresh fruits and vegetables come from the hotel
garden; milk, cream, and eggs are from the adjoining farm; and salmon
and lobster are from local river and sea.

A tour along the scenic Atlantic Drive, with a stop at the tiny village of Downings to see some of the famous Donegal tweed being hand-woven, is a worthwhile excursion.

Lough Swilly is an arm of the sea where the whole English fleet anchored in World War I. In 1607 a French ship anchored off Rathmullan to take aboard, with their families and retainers, Hugh O'Neill and Rory O'Donnell, leaders of the Irish forces defeated at the battle of Kinsale. They had been forced to flee into exile, an event known in history as "the flight of the Earls." The two earls are buried side by side in Rome beneath elaborate tombstones.

Price category: Moderate. *Proprietors:* Ann and Robin Fletcher. *Telephone:* (074) 58100. *Closed:* Mid-October to Easter. *Rooms:* 18, 15 with bath; 3 self-catering cottages; weekend breaks *Meals:* Breakfast, snacks, dinner for public; full license. *Children:* Baby-sitting; children's meals. *Facilities:* Lounge, TV room, cocktail bar, garden. *Activities:* Ocean swimming, tennis, squash, par-three golf, sailing, and game room at the hotel; boat rental nearby. *Credit cards:* Amex, Diners, Master, Visa. *U.S. agent:* RS. *How to get there:* The hotel is on Route R247. Guests can be met at the Belfast or Dublin airport.   [T]

RATHMULLAN HOUSE

The special delight of the Irish coast lies in this, that you are almost everywhere between the heather and the sea.

Stephen Gwynn, 1927

Rathmullan House is on the shores of Lough Swilly, with half a mile of sandy beach. Its glass-walled Pavilion Restaurant, in an unusual octagon shape, overlooks gardens that have won the National Garden Award for hotels. Both table d'hôte and à la carte meals are served, with lobster and Irish salmon being especially good. The cuisine is recommended in most food guides.

Wood and turf fires shed a glow over drawing room and library. Furnishings are a mix. Although mostly antique and traditional, some that aren't antique lack style. Fresh flowers and some stained-glass windows add to the country-house feeling.

It is an easy walk by road or along the beach to the historic village of Rathmullan. In 1798, Wolfe Tone was landed here after he had been captured on a French battleship in a sea-fight off Lough Swilly. He was the founder of the Society of United Irishmen formed to work toward

Irish freedom.

Price category: Inexpensive to expensive. *Proprietors:* Robin and Bob Wheeler. *Telephone:* (074) 58117 or 58188. *Closed:* Christmas to mid-March. *Rooms:* 21, 16 with bath. *Meals:* Luncheon, snacks, tea, dinner for public; full license. *Children:* Baby-sitting. *Facilities:* Drawing room, library, cocktail bar, garden. *Activities:* Ocean swimming, indoor pool, and sauna at the hotel; tennis, and riding nearby. *Credit cards:* Amex, Diners, Master, Visa. *U.S. agent:* Robert Reid. *How to get there:* The hotel is on Route R247. [T]

THE OLD RECTORY

> I am off on holiday next month to Donegal in northern Ireland, to the . . . lovliest country I know, a country of hills and hollows, of lakes and woods, of cliffs, mountains, rivers, inlets of sea, sands, ruined castles and memories from the beginning of the world.
>
> *AE (George Russell),* 1899

Maureen Brennan's greeting is so warm and her manner so gracious that you can't help but feel welcome at this Victorian house. It was built in 1876, with Gothic windows and stained glass popular at that time. Furnishings are comfortable, and beds have electric blankets.

The location of The Old Rectory, right in the village but in a cul-de-sac, is delightfully quiet. Across the road is nothing but the open beach where you can swim in Lough Swilly, a great salt-water inlet of the Atlantic Ocean.

North Donegal is an area of great beauty. Just north of Rathmullan is the Knockalla Coast Road, an eight-mile stretch of one of the most spectacular drives in Ireland.

Price category: Very inexpensive. *Proprietor:* Maureen Brennan. *Telephone:* (074) 58226. *Closed:* October to June. *Rooms:* 5 sharing baths. *Meals:* Dinner for guests; no license. *Children:* Baby-sitting. *Facilities:* Living room, garden. *Smoking:* Not permitted. *Activities:* Ocean swimming at the house; riding, tennis, and putting green nearby. *How to get there:* From Rathmullan center, turn north along the shore to The Old Rectory.

Rathnew, Wicklow

HUNTER'S HOTEL

The inns I have seen here are all better than we have
at home.

Sir Walter Scott, 1825

Hunter's Hotel is one of the very few in Ireland that is old enough to
have entertained Sir Walter; as his travels in Wicklow were extensive,

this is no doubt one of the inns he had in mind when he wrote the letter quoted above. It is an old coaching inn where horses were changed, the first stop from Dublin, a day's journey away. Lingering associations of those far-off days are evident when you walk through the Georgian doorway: interior shutters that fold back, antique lighting fixtures, old beams, iron and brass beds, marble-topped furniture, old prints. Guests gather around fireplaces where the flames are reflected in gleaming brass coal scuttles and fire fenders.

Hunter's draws top marks for its award-winning garden where palm trees combine with a great profusion of flowers. It makes a delightful setting for afternoon tea, with scones fresh from the oven and home-made strawberry jam. We loved a quaint sign that read "Ladies and gentlemen will not, and others must not, pick the flowers." Fresh fish from the sea, juicy roasts, and vegetables from the kitchen garden are offered in the dining room, recommended in many food guides. At Hunter's, five generations of one family have played host to overseas visitors, from those who came to Ireland by sailing packet to those who arrive by jet plane. We have friends who stopped for tea and stayed two days, then returned for another visit before leaving Ireland.

Price category: Moderate. *Proprietor:* Maureen Gelletlie. *Telephone:* (0404) 40106. *Rooms:* 18, 10 with bath. *Meals:* Breakfast, luncheon, snacks, tea, dinner; full license. *Children:* Baby-sitting. *Facilities:* Lounge, TV lounge, cocktail bar, garden. *Activities:* Riding, tennis, squash, ocean swimming, boat rental, deep-sea fishing, sailing, snorkeling, and canoeing nearby. *Credit cards:* Amex, Diners, Master, Visa. *U.S. agent:* Robert Reid Associates. *How to get there:* Rathnew is 3 miles northwest of the town of Wicklow.   [T]

TINAKILLY HOUSE

> Still south I went and west and south again,
> Through Wicklow from the morning till the night,
> And far from cities, and the sights of men,
> Lived with the sunshine, and the moon's delight.
> *John Millington Synge,* 1907

Over a century ago Tinakilly House was built for gracious living, and gracious living is what you'll find there today. Rooms in this house are truly spacious, from the impressive entrance lounge, with coffered ceiling and a balcony, to bedrooms with large bay windows, some of which offer a view of the distant Irish sea. Antiques in beautiful condition are augmented by new things of quality. Logs crackle in the fireplaces, and a grand piano is ready for a guest to play.

A feature of the house is the staircase, said to be a copy of the stairs on the Great Eastern, the largest ship on the seas when Captain Halpin, who built Tinakilly House, made his fame and fortune as its commander. With this ship he laid the first successful cable connecting Continental Europe with America. From around the world he brought back pine, mahogany, and bird's-eye maple that panel some of the rooms.

The dining room uses fish, meat, eggs, fruit, and vegetables produced mainly from nearby gardens, farms, and sea. The dinner menu offers some choices for each course. Ice cream is homemade.

It's a short drive to Glendalough, where, in the sixth century, St. Kevin established a monastic city whose fame as a center of learning drew students from all Europe. It is a tranquil place today, where history is enshrined in the ruins around its lakes.

Price category: Expensive. *Proprietors:* Bee and William Power. *Telephone:* (0404) 69274. *Rooms:* 14 with bath and telephone; 3-day reduction. *Meals:* Snacks, tea, and dinner (coat and tie preferred) for public; full license. *Children:* Not suitable for children under 7. *Facilities:* Drawing room, hall lounge, cocktail bar, garden. *Activities:* Riding, tennis, squash, ocean swimming, boat rental, sailing, snorkling, canoeing, and deep-sea, shore, and pier fishing nearby. *Credit cards:* Amex, Visa. *U.S. Agent:* Robert Reid Associates. *How to get there:* Rathnew is 3 miles northwest of the town of Wicklow. Tinakilly House is signposted on Route R750 between Wicklow and Rathnew.   [T]

Riverstown, Sligo

COOPERSHILL

> This romantic home of the olden days . . . is a house
> to be seen, not described; for its ancient charm, its old-
> world picturesqueness, and, above all, the sense of a
> past presence that seems to brood incumbent over its
> aged walls, are not to be given in prosaic print.
>
> *James Hissey,* 1889

Coopershill is an aristocrat of farmhouse lodgings, a great country
house clothed with the glamour of a luxurious past. Owned by the same
family since it was built in 1774, it is filled with comfortable old furniture, Oriental rugs, and antiques. Books and magazines abound, and
a log fire burns even in summer. Deer heads and antlers bedeck the
walls, legacy of a deer park once part of the demesne when Coopershill was in its eighteenth-century heyday. Older is a double-ended pad-
dle, which dates from before Christ, that was dug from a bog.

In a dining room where ancestors' portraits look down from the
walls, you will eat fresh country meals served from family silver on a
massive sideboard. Most bedrooms have half-tester or four-poster beds.
Cattle and sheep are raised on the farm's 500 acres.

Price category: Moderate. *Proprietors:* Brian and Lindy O'Hara.
Telephone: (071) 65108. *Closed:* November to mid-March. *Rooms:* 6
with bath. 3-day reduction. *Meals:* Dinner for guests; wine license.
Facilities: Drawing room, garden. *Smoking:* Permitted in drawing room
only. *Activities:* trout, pike, and perch fishing; riding; lake and ocean
swimming nearby. *Credit Cards:* Amex, Master, Visa. *U.S. agent:* Robert Reid. *How to get there:* From the south on N4 turn right onto the
road signposted to Riverstown, then take the second road left (after
about a mile) to Coopershill.   [T]

ABBEY HOTEL

We'll strive to please you every day.
William Shakespeare

Service and comfort get high marks at the Abbey Hotel in the town of Roscommon. The atmosphere here is that of a professional hotel, the best in town and well used by the residents of the area for weddings and civic dinners.

Its attractive restaurant serves good food, and pleasant modern bedrooms are comfortable, with good bathrooms that have both tub and shower. Set on well-kept spacious grounds with flower beds and mature trees, the hotel is run by its owners, with the help of a well-trained staff.

Beside the hotel and open to visitors is the ruin of an old abbey with a tomb said to be that of its thirteenth-century founder. The Abbey makes a convenient overnight stop, especially for those who prefer a hotel to a private-home guest house.

Price category: Moderate. *Proprietors:* Anya and Tom Grealy. *Telephone:* (093) 26240. *Rooms:* 20 with bath, telephone, TV, and tea-making. *Meals:* Luncheon, snacks, dinner for public; full license. *Facilities:* 2 Lounges, cocktail bar. *Activities:* Indoor pool, tennis, boat trips on the Shannon nearby. *Credit cards:* Amex, Diners, Master, Visa. *How to get there:* The hotel is on the main road in Roscommon.[T]

KELLY'S STRAND HOTEL

For now I am in a holiday humour.
William Shakespeare

When the Irish are in a holiday humor, their thoughts turn to Kelly's Strand Hotel. We have heard it called the best hotel in Ireland. If "best" means a hotel that keeps its customers happy, this one might well be called the best. Dubliners save all winter to take the family to "Kelly's" for an annual holiday; couples who haven't time to dash off to Spain drop in for a short winter break; singles who want a bit of socializing come any time.

The Strand was first recommended to us by a young Dublin career woman. When we asked if it had old world charm, she answered that it did not, then added, "Ah, but you want a bit of life now, don't you?" Three generations of Kellys have worked hard to develop this hotel, which offers its patrons activities galore.

Although this establishment started in a Victorian building, any Old-World ambience has long since been overwhelmed as Kelly's Strand Hotel has expanded. Today there are lounges, sun lounges, a solarium, a sauna, and rooms for television, cards, billiards, and snooker. Besides a ladies' hairdressing salon, you'll find a resident masseuse and a beauty therapist. For rainy days there are squash courts, an indoor swimming pool with a swimming coach, and indoor tennis courts. Dancing in season, sing-a-longs, and Irish plays keep you from having nothing to do in the evenings.

The hotel is right on the beach in this sunny corner of Ireland. Tennis courts and a putting green are on the grounds. In May and June, when bird life on the Saltee Islands is at its best, weekly trips are arranged, with a picnic lunch packed by the hotel.

The pleasures of Kelly's Strand Hotel are not confined to its many activities. The dining room is one of Ireland's best restaurants, recommended in all food guides. Fresh oysters, scallops, crabs, mussels, and other fish are from the nearby sea; beef, lamb, pork, and poultry are first quality; desserts are homemade. Snacks are served at the bars.

In summer, all rooms are booked by the week. It would be only by chance that a room would be available for a night or two at that time of year. If you are traveling with children, they'll find plenty of others to play with here.

An American we told about this hotel wrote recently, "Pure Irish fun. Food marvelous. Excellent value." If you want to meet the Irish at play, stay for a few days at Kelly's Strand Hotel.

Price category: Moderate. *Proprietor:* The Kelly family. *Telephone:* (053) 32114. *Closed:* Mid-December to mid-February. *Rooms:* 89, 85 with bath, all with telephone and TV; suitable for wheelchair guests. *Meals:* Luncheon, snacks, tea, dinner (jacket and tie) for guests; full license. *Children:* Baby-sitting and -listening, children's meals, playground. *Facilities:* Several lounges, card room, sun parlor, cocktail bar, public bar, game room, beauty salon, masseuse. *Activities:* Ocean swimming, indoor and outdoor tennis, putting green, squash, sauna, solarium, gymnasium, bowling, indoor and outdoor pools, bicycle rental, badminton, jogging track, dancing, movies, and sing-a-longs at the hotel. *How to get there:* Rosslare is on the coast south of the town of Wexford.

Rossnowlagh, Donegal

SAND HOUSE HOTEL

> O come hither! weeks together
> Let us watch the big Atlantic,
> Blue or purple, green or gurly,
> Dark or shining, smooth or frantic.
> > *William Allingham*, 1864

Here is a hotel in Allingham's beloved Donegal for those who love ocean beaches. Great waves from the Atlantic roll in along the 2 miles of broad, uncrowded sand, making this one of the best surfing beaches in Ireland. Rossnowlagh hosts the Irish intercounty championships.

The somewhat stark appearance of the outside of Sand House belies the warmth of the atmosphere within. Lounges are restful and congenial, enhanced by the glow of turf and log fires and the many antiques scattered about. There is a large game room with ping-pong and billiard tables. The public bar has great atmosphere, and here you are likely to chat with people who have vacation homes in the area. Bedrooms have been enlarged, and many are furnished with antiques. Ask for one facing the ocean, as these are the only rooms with a view; at the ground-floor level there is a sand dune between the hotel and the water. It is delightful to drift to sleep with the sound of the waves and the smell of the sea.

Members of the Britton family run this hotel with the help of a smiling, efficient, long-established staff. The Brittons are always talking with their guests, giving helpful advice when asked. This relaxed, friendly hotel with a fine spirit of warmth and goodwill is one of the best run in Ireland, for which it has won awards.

Price category: Expensive. *Proprietors:* Mary, David, and Conor Britton. *Telephone:* (072) 51777. *Closed:* Early October to Easter. *Rooms:* 40 with bath and telephone. *Meals: Luncheon, snacks, tea, dinner for public; full license. Facilities:* Lounge, TV room, sun lounge, cocktail bar, public bar. *Activities:* Ocean swimming, surfing, tennis, game room, free use of wind-surfers and canoes at the hotel. *Credit cards:* Amex, Master. *U.S. agent:* Selective Hotels. *How to get there:* Rossnowlagh is 8 miles north of the Leitrim border on Rt. R231.[T]

Schull, Cork

ARD NA GREINE

The little roads of Ireland
Stay forever in your mind.

Anonymous

One mile west of Schull, on one of Ireland's little roads, is a small country inn that was a once private house. In the friendly bar we met attractive people who had driven from as far as Bantry and Clonakilty to dine, among them Americans who had moved to Ireland. Nicely decorated bedrooms vary in size.

Schull is a fishing port where trawlers and smaller fishing boats go out to sea each day. People who find fresh seafood a treat come for the crab, lobster, prawns, salmon, mackerel, scallops, and other fish featured at Ard na Greine.

The gentle hills around are crowned with golden gorse—called "furze" in Ireland—that blooms throughout the year. There is an Irish saying that "Kissing is forbidden when the furze is not in bloom." Little roads trail out to Mizen Head signal station, where messages are transmitted to and received from ships at sea. Offshore stands the famous Fastnet Rock Lighthouse, the last piece of Irish soil seen by Irish emigrants to America. We read about it in headlines in July 1979, when a fierce storm descended unexpectedly upon boats sailing in the annual Fastnet Race from Cowes in England to around the lighthouse and back.

Price category: Expensive. *Proprietors:* Frank and Rhona O'Sullivan. *Telephone:* (028) 28181. *Closed:* November to Easter. *Rooms:* 7 with bath; ground-floor rooms. *Meals:* Snacks, tea, and dinner for public; full license. *Children:* Not suitable for those under twelve. *Facilities:* Lounge, cocktail bar, garden. *Activities:* Ocean swimming, sailing, deep-sea fishing, and tennis nearby. *Credit cards:* Amex, Diners, Visa. *U.S. agent:* Robert Reid Associates. *How to get there:* Ard na Greine is on Route R592, 1 mile west of Schull. [T]

Shanagarry, Cork

BALLYMALOE HOUSE

> There are certain places one visits and must leave part
> of one's heart. Ireland is foremost among these.
> *Leon Uris,* 1980

Like Ireland, Ballymaloe House is a place one visits and leaves part of one's heart. Its easygoing hospitality is one of the reasons; its restaurant, one of the few in Ireland given Michelin stars, is another. The simply decorated dining rooms are hung with paintings by Jack Yeats, brother of poet William Butler Yeats, and by later Irish artists, some contemporary. *Gourmet* magazine published an article about the food served by Myrtle Allen, who wrote *The Ballymaloe Cookbook.* Son Rory now runs the 600-acre farm, where tomatoes and mushrooms are grown commercially, that supplies almost everything for the table except fish. That comes daily from the fishing boats in Ballycotton, the next village. Sheep roam about keeping the lawn clipped, and guests may roam the farm as our son did when there one winter. He loved seeing the geese and ducks that hung aging on a back porch, symbolic of skilled husbandry.

On one end of the house is a Norman tower, part of a 1450 Geraldine castle. In places, the spiral stairs have crumbled and been replaced by ladders. The agile can scramble up to the ramparts and imagine watching from there the battle of Kinsale in 1602, which reshaped Irish history. Lord Mountjoy knighted the owner of Ballymaloe, John

Fitzgerald, after the battle. A famous harp made at Ballymaloe for Sir John is in the National Museum in Dublin.

Ballymaloe has entertained many famous guests in its day — among them William Penn and the philosopher Bishop Berkeley. There is a written account of Oliver Cromwell's riding to Ballymaloe with the earl of Orrery, who then owned it, while discussing the need to behead Charles II. But a memory of times far older than these hangs in Ballymaloe's front hall — elk antlers perfectly preserved in a bog and dug up on the farm. The last Irish elk died around 10,000 B.C., about when man first came to Ireland.

Furnishings are not fancy, although there are some very nice pieces in the old mansion. The lounge is the sort of place to make new friends. Guests sit around the fire as if at a private house party, getting up to make their own drinks on the honor system if no one else is around to do it for them. This is a warm and comfortable family home with the family still in it. Daughter-in-law Hazel Allen helps manage the inn, and daughter Wendy has an Irish-goods shop in another building.

The Ballymaloe Cooking School is run by Darina Allen, another daughter-in-law, at Kinoith, a beautiful Regency house. Darina worked for years with Myrtle Allen, who developed the Ballymaloe style of cooking and has lectured in the United States and France. This internationally-known school offers a 12-week certificate course, but you can take various courses that last from one day to one week. Send for the separate Brochure.

Price category: Moderate to expensive. *Proprietors:* Myrtle and Ivan Allen. *Telephone:* (021) 652531. *Closed:* December 24–26. *Rooms:* 30 with bath, and telephone; suitable for wheelchair guests. *Meals:* Snacks, and tea for guests; luncheon and dinner for public; full license. *Children:* Baby-sitting; children's meals; playground. *Facilities:* Lounge, TV room, sitting room, garden, craft shop. *Activities:* Outdoor pool, tennis, rowboat, and small golf course (all free for guests) at house; ocean swimming, riding, and deep-sea fishing nearby. *Credit cards:* Amex, Diners, Master, Visa. *U.S. agent:* Robert Reid. *How to get there:* Ballymaloe House is on Route R629 6 miles from Midleton and 2 miles beyond Cloyne. Guests can be met at the Cork airport or railway station.
[T]

BALLINCAR HOUSE HOTEL

> Cast a cold eye
> On life, on death;
> Horseman pass by.
>
> *William Butler Yeats's epitaph*

Literary pilgrims who want to visit the countryside so loved by William Butler Yeats will find Ballincar House on the road to "furthest Rosses." It is on the outskirts of Sligo town and 5 miles from Drumcliff churchyard, where the enigmatic epigraph above is carved on Yeats's headstone "under bare Ben Bulben's head." Yeats arranged the details of his burial years before his death, but when he died in France he was buried there. Ten years later his wishes were carried out, and he now lies in the churchyard where his great-grandfather was rector. All about this area are places with melodious names that recall the sound of his poetry—Lissadell, Innisfree, Glencar, Drumahair.

On 6 acres, the hotel was formerly the home of its present owner, Victor Blackwell. The public rooms are in the original building, and while they retain little Old World ambience, the hotel is pleasant and has a friendly staff. The dining room turns out good food, and bedrooms in a modern wing command a view across Sligo Bay to the Ox Mountains.

Rosses Point, just beyond the hotel, is identifiable with many of Yeats's poems. There you'll find Memory Harbor and the Metal Man, a statue in the harbor that marks the channel, both painted by Jack Yeats, renowned artist-brother of the poet.

Price category: Moderate. *Proprietor:* Victor Blackwell. *Telephone:* (071) 45361. *Closed:* December 23 to January 24. *Rooms:* 20 with bath, telephone, and TV; suitable for wheelchair guests. *Meals:* Breakfast, luncheon, dinner; full license. *Children:* Baby-sitting and -listening. *Facilities:* Lounge, TV lounge, cocktail bar, garden. *Activities:* Tennis, squash, and sauna at the hotel; ocean swimming, boat trips, and riding nearby. *Credit cards:* Amex, Diners, Master, Visa. *U.S. agent:* RS. *How to get there:* The hotel is on Route L18 between Sligo and Rosses Point.   [T]

Spiddal, Galway

ARDMOR

> The great waves of the Atlantic sweep storming on
> the way,
> Shining green and silver with the hidden herring shoal.
>
> *Eva Gore-Booth*

Great waves of the Atlantic were storming the coast bordering Ardmor on the sunny day we arrived, a magnificent sight, a place to watch the sea in all its moods.

The Irish spirit of friendliness is very much a reality at this modern home, where many Irish visitors return year after year. In a large room with books — a combination lounge and dining room — guests exchange their day's experiences. Because the land slopes, some bedrooms are on the entrance level and others are downstairs at the garden level. All are larger than average for a modern house. Best are those upstairs that face the ocean, with a gorgeous view of it across colorful gardens.

Guests can bask in the sun on either a garden terrace or a sun deck. Paths wind through the gardens down to the shore, where bathing is good on days when the sea is not so rough. Vera Feeney will make all arrangements for you to go to the Aran Islands. At her suggestion, we left our car at her house and had the free bus to the boat pick us up at, and return us to, her door. You can do the same whether your visit to Aran is for the day or for several nights.

In Spiddal, Mairtin Standun's shop, known for good value, has one of the largest stocks of Irish goods in the country.

Price category: Very inexpensive. *Proprietor:* Mrs. Vera Feeney. *Telephone:* (091) 83145. *Closed:* December through February. *Rooms:* 6 with bath; ground floor rooms. *Meals:* Dinner for guests; no license. *Children:* Baby-sitting. *Facilities:* Lounge, garden, laundry. *Activities:* Ocean swimming at the house; boat trips to the Aran Islands nearby. *How to get there:* Ardmor is on Route R336 just west of Spiddal.

CHURCH VIEW HOUSE

> Roscommon itself is a necklace of somnolent lakes
> opening off the River Shannon.
> *Max Caulfield,* 1973

A long, flower-bordered driveway leads to serene, secluded Church View House, where you'll be greeted with warm hospitality by Harriet Cox.

Antique furniture harmonizes with the old building, a Georgian house that has had an addition. A spacious living room, with big comfortable chairs and couch to curl up on, invites evenings of conversation with other guests. From the large, sunny dining room, where everyone dines together at one table, French doors lead to a terrace that has garden furniture and beds of flowers. Large windows in the bedrooms show views over fields to Kilglass Lake, which borders the farm. A rowboat is there for the use of guests.

Anyone who wants to trace Roscommon ancestors should go to St. John's County Heritage Centre in Strokestown.

Price category: Very inexpensive. *Proprietors:* The Cox family. *Telephone:* (078) 33047. *Closed:* November through March except by reservation. *Rooms:* 7, 1 with bath. *Meals:* Dinner or supper for guests: wine license. *Facilities:* Living room, garden. *Activities:* Rowboat and riding on farm; boat trips on the Shannon nearby. *How to get there:* If coming into Strokestown from the north, take left signposted Kilglass Lake and find arrows to the house.

TAHILLA COVE

> Your geography tells you that you are on the coast of
> Kerry, but your subliminal consciousness keeps whis-
> pering to you directly you set foot on the magic strand
> that you are landed on a paradise of the South Pacific.
> *Twells Brex*

The beautiful setting on the shores that enchanted the nineteenth-century journalist quoted above is enough to make a visit to Tahilla Cove
worthwhile. The waters of the Gulf Stream warm the coast and its tropical foliage. Many visitors are surprised to find palm trees here, but
they are not uncommon in this part of Ireland.

Guest rooms are in two simple houses on 12 acres that stretch along
the sparsely settled bay. Many antiques are among the furnishings. This
is a place for quiet relaxation; the late President Childers of Ireland,
who was a friend of the owners', came here just before he took office,
to rest and recover from the campaign. Guests swim at Tahilla Cove's
pebbled beach and can rent boats to moor at its private pier.

For an otherworldly experience, drive through Ballaghbeama Gap,
where great stretches of mountainous moorland carpeted with heather
are silent but for the call of a wild bird or the bleating of the few sheep
dotting the mountainsides. It is truly the back of beyond. The road
through the gap will bring you to a little road around Caragh Lake,
where you may meet a donkey out for a solitary stroll. From there you
can circle the Ring of Kerry to return to Tahilla Cove.

Price category: Inexpensive. *Proprietors:* James, Deirdre, and Dolly
Waterhouse. *Telephone:* (064) 45204. *Closed:* Mid-October through
March. *Rooms:* 9 with bath; ground-floor rooms. *Meals:* Snacks, tea,
and dinner for public; full license. *Facilities:* Lounge, TV lounge, bar,
garden. *Activities:* Ocean swimming at the house; tennis, fishing, boat
rental, deep-sea fishing, boat trips, and riding nearby. *Credit cards:*
Amex, Diners, Master, Visa. *How to get there:* The house is on the Ring
of Kerry, Route N70, 5 miles east of Sneem.

AN GRIANAN

> In Ireland there are no strangers, only friends you
> haven't met before.
>
> *Anonymous*

If you would like to meet the Irish people, this is a splendid place to do so. An Grianan is a residential Adult Education College where you can take five-day courses ranging from literature, music, and calligraphy to cooking, horticulture, and bridge. Friends of ours, an American doctor and his wife who visit Ireland yearly, come here for a week or two each summer to take painting courses. You might enjoy Irish Heritage, Yoga, or Care and Repair of Antiques.

Originally a stately home built about 1780, the estate was entrusted in 1954 to the Irish Countrywomen's Association by the W. K. Kellogg Foundation of America, for the "health, education, and welfare of the people of Ireland." Wings have been added for bedrooms, many of them singles, and for elaborate facilities such as the modern demonstration kitchen, art studio, dance room, theater, and gymnasium.

Guests arrive late Monday afternoon and leave after lunch Friday. The staff is welcoming, and you'll be bound to meet the other visitors and discuss the day's happenings in the large living room or the cocktail bar. An Grianan receives tributes for its traditional Irish cuisine. (Special diets can be accommodated.) It's a great place for a single traveler and an inexpensive way to travel.

Special lectures are arranged nightly, and Thursday night is renowned for musical entertainment and an impromptu concert. Guests frequently make the one-hour trip to Dublin to attend the Abbey Theatre. For those who cannot spend five days, one-day demonstrations are organised at various times. Send to An Grianan for its program of courses.

Price category: Inexpensive *Manager:* Celine Fanning and Jane McAuley. *Telephone:* (041) 22119. *Closed:* Christmas. *Rooms:* 49 sharing baths. *Meals:* All meals for guests. *Children:* Not suitable under 16. *Facilities:* Drawing room, cocktail bar, garden. *Activities:* Gymnasium and sauna at An Grianan. *How to get there:* By train or bus to Drogheda (pronounced Draw' hedda), then taxi to An Grianan (pronounced On Greenawn). Termonfechin is on the coast on Route R166, 5 miles north of Drogheda.

BALLYNAHOW CASTLE FARM

> Oh, come for a while among us,
> And give us the friendly hand
> And you'll see that old Tipperary
> Is a loving and gladsome land.
> *Eva Marie Kelly,* 1855

We sat in front of a turf fire enjoying good conversation and the tea and scones Mary Finn brought us when we unexpectedly arrived at Ballynahow Castle Farm one afternoon. Jim Finn joined us after happening into the house from the farm; he couldn't resist telling us about the history of the area when he realized our interest, though he's a busy man. Raising both dairy and beef cattle, he is also a photographer and offers something unusual to guests—the use of a darkroom for those who know how to develop film. He also has made video tapes of Ireland that guests can enjoy in the TV room.

The house is over 150 years old, furnished with some antiques and with books for browsing. A modern bathroom for guests has a stall shower as well as a tub. Bedrooms come with electric blankets.

On the farm near the house is the turreted ruin of Ballynahow Castle, a National Monument. Built by the Purcells in the sixteenth century, it is five stories high and one of the few in Ireland that is round. Two ceilings are preserved, one flat corbelled and the other vaulted. There is a "murder hole" above the door from which boiling oil was poured on intruders.

Price category: Very inexpensive. *Proprietors:* Mary and Jim Finn. *Telephone:* (0504) 21297. *Closed:* November through April. *Rooms:* 4 sharing baths. *Meals:* Dinner for guests; no license. *Children:* Baby-sitting. *Facilities:* Sitting room, garden, photographer's darkroom, painting studio. *Activities:* Indoor pool nearby. *How to get there:* The house is signposted on Route T503, three miles west of Thurles in the village of Ballycahill. [T]

BALLYGARRY HOTEL

> It is very noticeable in Ireland how close the hills, fields, and trees are to the towns.
>
> *Chiang Yee,* 1953

With views of hills, fields, and trees, the BallyGarry Hotel is just outside the town of Tralee. The atmosphere is more that of a town hotel than a country house, but its owners provide a welcoming atmosphere and take a personal interest in the comfort of their guests.

The hotel is nicely decorated in soft colors and pretty fabrics, with an occasional antique piece for accent. Ask for a bedroom in the back—which will have a view across the fields to the mountains—as the hotel is set close to a busy main road. Rooms are named for areas in Kerry.

The dining room has established a reputation for good food and uses all fresh produce when possible. Guests and local patrons congregate in the congenial bar-lounge, attractive with a log fire, where a pianist plays on weekends in season. There is no resident's lounge. The second-floor deck is a pleasant place to sit out in the sun and enjoy the view.

The BallyGarry Hotel is a good stopping place for those who want to try the new Tralee Golf Course, designed by Arnold Palmer. Horse racing in Ireland is great fun, and Tralee has a track. You can get a calendar from the Irish Tourist Board for the racing schedule.

Price category: Moderate. *Proprietors:* Owen and Pearl McGillicuddy. *Telephone:* (066) 23322. *Closed:* 1 week at Christmas. *Rooms:* 16 with bath, telephone, TV, and tea-making. *Meals:* Dinner for public; full license. *Children:* Baby-sitting, playroom, playground. *Facilities:* Cocktail lounge, garden. *Activities:* Tennis, ocean swimming, sailing lessons, deep-sea fishing, and riding nearby. *Credit cards:* Master, Visa. *How to get there:* The hotel is on Route N21, the Killarney road, a mile south of Tralee.

[T]

Tyrellspass, Westmeath

VILLAGE HOTEL

> The village inn, Sir, is a pleasant place
> Where man finds company, good ale and grace.
> *John Nicholas*

The Village Hotel is part of a crescent of buildings constructed around a village green in 1800 by the Countess of Belvedere. Tyrellspass has more of architectural interest than most Irish villages.

We arrived at the small hotel during Sunday lunch, a weekly event that draws residents from miles around, and no wonder! A first course of pâté, seafood chowder, prawns, fruit cocktail, or cream soup was being served. A joint of roast beef and a baked ham anchored a bounteous buffet, where Indian curry, barbecued beef, fried chicken, vegetables, and salads were attractively presented. Fresh fish was on order, and all was followed by a selection from a dessert table. At the same time, a really good choice of light fare was available in the bar. It was obvious that the Piersons take pride in serving good food.

Busy as he was, affable Peter Pierson found time to show us around. A good-sized bar-lounge, with open fire, partly separated from the bar itself so that it has somewhat the feeling of a living room, attracts locals and visitors alike. Small but comfortable bedrooms had just been refurbished with hotel furniture of traditional design. An attitude of friendly hospitality prevailed. Travelers would find this hotel a useful place to spend a night while traveling between Dublin and the west. Neat Tyrellspass is an interesting village in which to take a walk before dinner.

Price category: Inexpensive. *Proprietors:* Brenda and Peter Pierson. *Telephone:* (044) 23171. *Closed:* Christmas. *Rooms:* 10 with bath and tea-making. TV available. *Meals:* Dinner for public; full license. *Children:* Baby-sitting. *Facilities:* Lounge-bar. *Credit cards:* Amex, Diners, Master, Visa. *U.S. agent:* RS. *How to get there:* The hotel is on the main Dublin-Galway road, Route N6. [T]

BLENHEIM HOUSE

In all the world there is no land
With spots more beautiful and grand
Than the bonny dales of Ireland.
Mildred Hobbs, 1925

Blenheim House, a patrician mansion built in 1763, stands in beautiful grounds at the end of a long driveway. Behind the dignified exterior you'll find a large drawing room where green velvet-covered chairs keep company with a Victorian sofa around a fire. Another wood fire glows in the dining room, where guests sit together at a rosewood Victorian table. Each airy bedroom has its own modern bathroom.

The Fitzmaurices are antique collectors. In the house you will find such pieces as inlaid pedestals now used for flower arrangements, old French sleigh beds, cheval mirrors, chaise longues, and early Beleek.

If you are coming to Waterford to tour the famous glass factory, Claire will reserve your tour. In season, many local pubs and hotels feature evenings of Irish music and dancing. There are many restaurant choices for dinner.

Price category: Very inexpensive. *Proprietor:* Mrs. Claire Fitzmaurice. *Telephone:* (051) 74115. *Rooms:* 6 with bath. *Children:* Baby-sitting. *Facilities:* Drawing room, garden. *Activities:* Ocean swimming, sailing, surfing, boat rental, river cruising, and squash nearby. *Mailing address:* Blenheim Heights, Waterford, County Waterford. *How to get there:* From Waterford take Route R683 southeast. Turn onto Route R688 and almost right away you'll see a sign for Blenheim Heights, where you'll find Blenheim House signposted.

DERRYNANE

A morsel of genuine history is a thing so rare as to be always valuable.

Thomas Jefferson

History-loving Americans, especially Civil War buffs, will find this bed-and-breakfast lodging of great interest. It was the boyhood home of General Thomas Francis Meagher, commander of New York's "Fighting 69th" regiment at the first battle of Bull Run. His father was mayor of Waterford, and the house was built in 1820 by his maternal grandfather. Meagher was condemned to death at the age of twenty-three for his part as a leader in the ill-fated Irish revolutionary movement of 1848. His sentence was commuted to life imprisonment in Van Diemen's Land (Tasmania), from which he escaped to America after three years. He toured the country lecturing and then became a lawyer and editor. After the first battle of Bull Run, Meagher raised New York's volunteer Irish Brigade, which foughtat Yorktown, Richmond, Antietam, and Fredericksburg, where he was wounded. After the war, President Andrew Johnson appointed him governor of the Montana Territory.

A glimmer of Derrynane's former elegance shows in the high ceilings and in the antique furniture in the sunny dining room. The furnishings of all the other rooms are very basic, very clean, and plain. We recommend this only to those who are used to traveling the bed-and-breakfast route. No dinner is served—not a problem as the location is close to downtown restaurants—nor is there any license to serve spirits. Derrynane is just a few steps from Reginald's tower, a massive circular stone fortress built in 1003, with walls 10 feet thick, a visible remnant of Viking occupation that has survived almost a thousand years of turbulent history. It is now the civic museum.

Price category: Very inexpensive. *Proprietor:* Eilish Sullivan. *Telephone:* (051) 75179. *Closed:* November through February. *Rooms:* 8, 1 with bath. *Facilities:* TV room. *Mailing address:* 19, The Mall, Waterford, County Waterford. *How to get there:* Derrynane is in the center of town, a block from the Tower Hotel. It's a twenty-minute walk from the railway station, but taxis are available.

FOXMOUNT FARM

> It was a little like living at home without any of the
> cares of home life.
>> *Robert Gibbings,* 1941

Pursuing the most appealing of Ireland's farmhouse lodgings has led us to many friendly homes, but few have been as attractive as Foxmount Farm. Floral chintz and rose-velvet chairs and sofa are grouped around a tile-faced hearth in the drawing room. Bedrooms have antique furniture.

Dinner includes produce fresh from the garden, as well as home baking and homemade ice cream, with coffee following in the drawing room, where Mr. Kent, an avid fan of American as well as Continental sports, joined us before the fire. Tea and cookies are brought in every evening before bedtime. If you telephone or write ahead to reserve a room, tell Mrs. Kent if you'll want dinner, as she must know by early afternoon. Because we arrived, unexpected, in late afternoon, we went to the Suir Inn at Cheek Point on Waterford harbor. It's a charming country pub that offers an assortment of salads and hot dishes.

As we drove up the driveway leading to the Georgian house, a horse and pony in a pasture trotted to the fence to inspect us. Houseguests may ride these at no charge and may also use a hard tennis court. Mrs. Kent will book a tour of the Waterford glass factory for you. Just 6 miles away is Tramore's superb sandy beach, and even closer is the quaint and lively fishing village of Dunmore East. You'll be well pleased with Foxmount Farm.

Price category: Very inexpensive. *Proprietor:* Margaret Kent. *Telephone:* (051) 74308. *Closed:* Late September through March. *Rooms:* 5 with 2 shared baths. *Meals:* Dinner for guests; no license. *Children:* Baby-sitting, playroom, table tennis, and pony rides. *Facilities:* Drawing room, garden. *Activities:* Tennis at the farm, ocean swimming, sailing, surfing, boat rental, river cruising, and squash nearby. *Mailing address:* Foxmount Farm, Halfway House, Waterford, County Waterford. *How to get there:* From Waterford take the road toward Dunmore East. After about 4 miles take the left fork toward Passage East. Foxmount Farm is signposted on the right about 2 miles before Passage East.

WATERFORD CASTLE HOTEL

> Here moved on,
> In stately minuet lords, with doublets slashed
> And ladies rustling in the stiff brocade.
> *Lydia Signourney,* 1856

This Norman castle was built about 1160 by the Earl of Pembroke and was more recently inhabited by the nineteenth-century poet Edward Fitzgerald, translator of the Rubaiyat of Omar Khayyam. Italian Princess Caracciolo, his lineal descendant, lived here until the 1970's. Now it's a luxury hotel.

On an island of three-hundred lush acres in the River Suir, the massive stone building exhibits gargoyles of great antiquity. You'll enter the Great Hall, where soaring walls of stone are panelled in Elizabethan oak and where Gothic arches lead to other rooms. The flames that leap in the huge welcoming stone fireplace are fed by logs from the surrounding woodlands.

A stately oak-panelled dining room is resplendent with an ornate plastered ceiling and carved oak fireplace bearing the Fitzgerald crest. China is Wedgewood etched with a reproduction of the castle, and crystal is Waterford engraved with the castle's crest. Fruit and vegetables are grown organically in five acres of greenhouses, and herds of organically fed cattle, sheep, and deer supply beef, lamb, and venison.

The standard bedrooms are attractively furnished with antique reproductions. Deluxe bedrooms and suites, one with Italian furniture, offer the real thing. Antique tiles and beautiful Italian bath fixtures embellish many bathrooms. If you want sybaritic luxury, ask for the Presidential Suite.

Numerous oil paintings of horses reflect the owners' interest—seventeen horses and ponies are available for guests to ride along the island's bridle trails. Three-day events are planned, and hunting can be arranged. The hotel can be reached only by a two-minute ride on a ferry owned by the castle.

Price category: Very expensive. *Manager;* Richard Sherwood. *Telephone:* (051) 78203. *Fax:* (051) 72392 *Rooms:* 14 rooms with bath, telephone, and TV; 5 suites. Christmas and New Year's programs. *Meals:* Luncheon and dinner for public (with a no-smoking section). *Children:* Baby-sitting. *Facilities:* Great hall, lounge, conservatory, garden. *Activities:* Tennis, indoor pool, salmon and trout fishing from shore, riding, pheasant and duck shooting, and clay pigeon shooting at the hotel; ocean swimming, water skiing, deep-sea fishing, hunting and polo (including instruction) nearby. *Credit cards:* Amex, Diners, Master, Visa. *U.S. agent:* BTH. *How to get there:* The hotel is signposted 1 1/2 miles south of Waterford city on the Dunmore East road.   [T]

THE HUNTSMAN

> This wild tangle of mountain and glen, this honeycomb
> of sea and land, stretching far into the Atlantic . . .
> called the Waterville Promontory.
>
> *Twells Brex*

A wild tangle of mountain and glen, a honeycomb of sea and land, still surround the village of Waterville as they did almost a hundred years ago when the English journalist Brex was there. The village surrounds the Huntsman on three sides. Just across a narrow road, on the fourth side, is a sandy beach.

On the famous Ring of Kerry, The Huntsman is a well-known restaurant recommended by Michelin. Much less well-known is that you can also stay overnight here, and your bedroom will cost less than your dinner. We seldom recommend lodging that offers no sitting room or lounge for its guests. However, Waterville is such a busy little place that you do not need a lounge in which to spend the evening. During most of the months that The Huntsman is open, daylight continues until 10:00 P.M. You will want to walk about the village, dropping in and out of pubs, hotels, and shops, and take a stroll along the beach.

There are two bedrooms, each with a bath and shower. A Continental breakfast that includes fruit and cereal is served in the rooms and can be taken out to a garden terrace that is protected from the wind. There are also two 2-bedroom, self-catering apartments that sleep five, each with fireplace, television set, and washing machine. These are usually occupied by the week in high season but are rented out by the night otherwise.

Fresh sea food and local lamb are two features of the restaurant, and take-out service is provided by its gourmet delicatessen. In the winter, the Hunts operate a restaurant in La Quinta, California.

Price category: Very inexpensive. *Proprietors:* Deirdre and Raymond Hunt. *Telephone:* (0667) 4124. *Closed:* November to mid-March. *Rooms:* 2 with bath; ground-floor rooms; 2 2-bedroom self-catering apartments. *Meals:* Luncheon, snacks, dinner for public; full license. *Facilities:* Garden terrace. *Activities:* Ocean swimming in front of The Huntsman; riding, deep-sea fishing, boat rides and boat rental nearby. *Credit cards:* Amex, Diners, Master, Visa. *How to get there:* From Waterville center, start north along the shore road. The Huntsman is on the right.

FERRYCARRIG HOTEL

A plentuous place is Ireland for hospitable cheer,
translated from Irish by Samuel Ferguson, 1856

The Ferrycarrig Hotel is a hospitable, cheerful place, thanks to its gregarious manager, Matt Britton. He meets all his guests and does everything possible to make their visits memorable.

The hotel is far more attractive inside than you'd guess from seeing its stark modern exterior from the highway. And the setting on the banks of the wide Slaney Estuary is lovely. Landscaped lawns and gardens stretch down to the water's edge. Groups of tables and chairs are placed there, protected by cleverly designed windbreaks so you can enjoy sitting out, no matter the direction of the wind. A walk along the water on the grounds leads to the ruin of Ferrycarrig Castle and a National Heritage Park.

Bedrooms are decorated in an attractive modern style, some larger than others. All enjoy views across the estuary where rare waterfowl abound. Open a window and your room will fill with their sounds. In a conservatory restaurant, which faces the same view, we enjoyed excellent food from an extensive menu. Our seafood chowder was as good as any in our native New England. Frequently, local musicians play semi-classical and show numbers during dinner. There is no sitting room, but the large bar-lounge is bright and comfortable—a place where we felt at ease while reading without drinking.

Price category: Expensive. *Manager;* Matt Britton. *Telephone:* (053)22999. *Rooms:* 40 with bath, telephone, TV, and tea-making. *Meals:* Lunch and dinner for public (with a no-smoking section); full license. *Facilities:* Cocktail lounge, garden. *Activities:* Tennis at the hotel; ocean swimming and riding nearby. *Credit cards:* Amex, Diners, Master, Visa. *How to get there:* The hotel is on the banks of the Slaney Estuary, 2 to 3 miles from Wexford on Rt R741.   [T]

KNOCKROBIN COUNTRY HOUSE

> Generally the inhabitants of Wicklow are very intelli-
> gent, and their country well cultivated, especially near
> the coast. The low mountains and the numerous well-
> built houses give the district a very agreeable aspect.
> *Chevalier De La Tocnaye,* 1797

Knockrobin is an early Victorian house near the coast, refurbished with sunny colors and pretty floral fabrics and furnished with family antiques, many of them also Victorian. Thoughtful notes such as fresh fruit and mineral water in the bedrooms are welcoming.

Alison Andrew-Schlepers was catering director for a large firm in London before she and her Dutch husband decided to open a restaurant and guest house in Wicklow where she was born. Many of her recipes are adapted from her great-grandmother's Victorian cook books, with game a feature in season.

Roast venison is served in thin slices with crumbs of crisp bacon and a trickle of red currant jelly. Gerhard grows the vegetables organically. Tempting, old-fashioned desserts seldom seen on menus include syllabubs and rich rice, apple, and bread puddings with real whipped cream. Guests gather afterwards in the firelit drawing room for coffee and little macaroons.

Peacocks roam the extensive grounds, from which you can walk to Broadlough Bird Sanctuary in five minutes. We recommend a drive to Glendalough and from there a circle tour through the rugged Wicklow hills. Take Wicklow Gap to Blessington and return by Sally Gap.

Price category: Moderate to expensive. *Proprietors:* Alison and Gerhard Andrew-Schlepers. *Telephone:* (0404) 69424. *Closed:* 2 weeks in February. *Rooms:* 4 with bath, telephone, TV, and tea-making. *Meals:* Luncheon, tea and dinner to public by reservation (except Monday); wine license. *Facilities:* Drawing room, garden. *Activities:* Tennis, clay-pigeon shooting, bicycle rental at house; riding, ocean swimming, boat rental, deep-sea, pier and shore fishing nearby. *Credit cards:* Amex, Master, Visa. *How to get there:* Knockrobin is on Route N11 between Rathnew and Wicklow.

OLD RECTORY

> The scenery of Wicklow . . . possesses a genial glowing luxury . . . its beauties seem *alive*. It blooms; it blossoms.
>
> *Sir Jonah Barrington,* 1828

To tour the lush scenery of County Wicklow, you'd do well to stay at the Old Rectory. From it you can walk to the lively waterfront of the quaint harbor town of Wicklow. The decor of the serene old house is attractive with Laura Ashley fabrics, antique furniture, original watercolors, black marble mantels and high plasterwork ceilings. All bedrooms are thoughtfully supplied with mineral water, nice toiletries, and packets of information about Wicklow and a large-scale map of the area. You may have breakfast in bed at no extra charge.

The Old Rectory is best known for its restaurant, recommended by many international dining guides. The cuisine is basically French, with special Irish dishes. Specialties include duck in filo pastry, stuffed salmon, and fresh crab. Among the interesting first courses are turnip and bacon soup and cheese and herb fondue. Desserts are quite irresistible — profiteroles with hot chocolate sauce, honey barm-brack flambéed with whiskey and topped with whipped cream, and "Champagne Charlie" ice cream among them. Vegetarians are welcomed.

This country house–restaurant is very personally run. The food, prepared by Linda from fresh local materials, is served by Paul in the candlelit dining room. The wine list is carefully selected. You may take your coffee beside a log fire in the drawing room if you like. It's an especially good choice for those who don't want to drive, as you can come by train or bus. Bicycles can be rented in the town.

Price category: Moderate. *Proprietors:* Paul and Linda Saunders. *Telephone:* (0404) 67048. *Closed:* November through March. *Rooms:* 4 with bath, telephone, TV, and tea making. 2-night reduction. *Meals:* Dinner for the public by reservation; wine license. *Facilities:* Drawing room, garden. *Activities:* Tennis, riding, ocean swimming, sailing, and deep-sea, pier, and shore fishing nearby. *How to get there:* The Old Rectory is on Route N11 in Wicklow. Guests can be met at the Wicklow railway station, a five-minute walk away. The bus from Dublin and Arklow stops close by. [T]

INDEX OF INNS WITH RATES

The prices in this index were those for two people in high season in 1988 and include tax and service. Unless otherwise indicated, they included breakfast (usually a full breakfast but occasionally a Continental breakfast, which, in Ireland, usually includes juice, dry cereal, and a variety of breads). Rates are given in Irish pounds, with their dollar equivalents in parentheses. The dollar exchange rate was figured at $1.45 to the pound. Where two prices are given, they are for the lowest- and highest-priced double rooms. Many establishments offer lower prices off season. A few charge more during holidays and special events. Most give reductions to children. Always ask for the current rates before you make reservations.

The following abbreviations are used:

EP = European Plan — no breakfast

MAP = Modified American Plan — rates include dinner and breakfast

Send us your name and address...
...and we'll send you a free gift.

If you purchased this book, we'd like your name and address for our mailing list. Just supply the information below, and we'll send you your free gift.

I purchased this book at:

☐ Atticus
☐ Barnes & Noble
☐ B. Dalton Booksellers
☐ Bookland
☐ Books Inc.
☐ Crown Books
☐ Encore Books
☐ Hunter's Books
☐ J.K. Gill

☐ Kroch's & Brentano's
☐ Lauriats
☐ Marshall Field & Co.
☐ Paperback Booksmith
☐ Readmore
☐ Stacy's
☐ Taylors
☐ Upstart Crow & Co.
☐ Waldenbooks

Other:_____   (City)_____

I purchased this book on (approximate date):_____

Please send my free gift to:

Name:_____

Street or Box:_____

City_____State_____Zip_____

Please mail to:
The Compleat Traveler, c/o Burt Franklin & Co., Inc.
235 East 44th St., New York, N.Y. 10017 U.S.A.   Ireland

Limit: One per customer.   **Limited time offer.**

THE COMPLEAT TRAVELER'S READER REPORT

To: *The Compleat Traveler*
   c/o Burt Franklin & Co., Inc.
   P.O. Box 856
   New York, New York 10014, U.S.A.

Dear Compleat Traveler:

I have used your book in _____ (country or region).
I would like to offer the following ☐ new recommendation, ☐ comment,
☐ suggestion, ☐ criticism, ☐ or complaint about:

Name of Country Inn or Hotel:

_____

Address: _____

_____

Comments:

Day of my visit: _____   Length of stay: _____

From (name): _____

Address _____

_____ Telephone: _____